# CHANGING FACES, CHANGING PLACES

Bletchley and Woburn Sands district

1945-1970

**Ted Enever**

The
Book
Castle

*To the memory of George and Ivy Whittaker,*
*my parents-in-law, and Donald Gilks.*

Also by Ted Enever:
Cockney Kid and Countrymen.
Britain's Best Kept Secret - Ultra's base at Bletchley Park.

First published October 2002 by
The Book Castle
12 Church Street
Dunstable
Bedfordshire LU5 4RU

© Ted Enever 2002

ISBN 1 903747 20 1

Typeset & Designed by Priory Graphics
Printed by Antony Rowe Ltd.,
Chippenham, Wiltshire

Front Cover:
*Top: Grandfather Fred Enever in 1946.*
*Main Picture: Part of Bletchley Road's main shopping area in the 1960s.*
*Bottom: Four of Aspley Guise's young ladies in the 1950s.*

Back Cover:
*Top: The Bedford-Bletchley motor-train in 1951.*
*Middle: Terry Wright as a young apprentice in 1952.*
*Bottom: Frost's Garden Centre at Woburn Sands in the 1950s.*

# CONTENTS

**About the author....**

Ted Enever was educated at Bedford Modern School and entered journalism in 1951 with the Bletchley District Gazette. After his two years National Service in the army he continued his career as a freelance, combining this with work in the family greengrocery business. He returned to staff journalism in 1964. In 1967 he became editor of the Bucks Standard at Newport Pagnell before joining Marshall Cavendish, the London based international publishers, as deputy managing editor. In 1971 Mr Enever joined the Inner London Education Authority as managing editor and publications which he launched and controlled won many national trade awards. In 1987 he was appointed Director of Public Affairs with the British Dental Association before joining Milton Keynes Development Corporation, two years later, where he managed all media relations and was involved in a wide range of marketing, ceremonial and public relations activities.

Retiring when the Corporation was wound up in 1992, Ted Enever was a founder member of the Bletchley Park Trust and served as its chief executive and a Trustee in its formative years. He still plays an active part in the Trust's fund raising activities and is author of a successful book detailing the setting up of the wartime code-breaking centre, 'Britain's Best Kept Secret – Ultra's Base at Bletchley Park.' He was recently made a patron of the Bletchley Park Trust.

A keen gardener and sportsman, Ted Enever is a past president of Bletchley St Martin's Bowls Club. Married with two children, Ted, wife Barbara and daughter Rachel now live in Bletchley after having homes in Bow Brickhill for many years. Ted's son, Mark, still lives in the village. Recently the family extended its interest in racing by becoming co-owners of two horses, both trained by Peter Harris at his stables in Tring.

# INTRODUCTION

Following the publication of 'Cockney Kid and Countrymen' early in March of 2001, I was urged by many of its readers to carry on with the story of life in Woburn Sands and Aspley Guise in the years immediately following the Second World War. A year on, here is my modest attempt to meet those demands for a sequel.

'Changing Faces, Changing Places' covers the period from 1945 to the late 1960s, when the massive development of Milton Keynes came off the drawing board. In addition to revisiting in word and picture form the villages of Woburn Sands and Aspley Guise, I also recall schooling in Bedford. Then comes the earlier part of what I call my Bow Brickhill years for, following my marriage to Barbara, a Bow Brickhill girl, in 1957, we lived in that village until we moved to Bletchley in the 1980s. As a backdrop to these recollections is an overview of the rapid expansion of Bletchley between 1945 and the mid-1960s, when the announcement to build Milton Keynes was made.

This rapid expansion – a 'bigger, brighter, better Bletchley' as the policy was known – was synonymous with the general wish of the country to move forward into a new era of prosperity following six hard years of war. Part of that new dream of prosperity was to manifest itself in the desire for everyone to own a car, and as vehicle ownership grew and lifestyles generally became more mobile, so the village communities began to change at the expense of the developing towns.

As well as the individual memories of villagers and Bletchley people recorded within this text, I hope I might also convey the shift in the social pattern of life which has so radically changed the face of North Bucks over the past fifty years. Milton Keynes itself is now well over thirty years old and has, in the main, proved a very successful undertaking. Though billed initially as a multi-centred city, with Bletchley, Stony Stratford and Wolverton sharing equal prominence with Central Milton Keynes, Kingston and Westcroft as centres, this is one aspect that has gone awry. Just as in a conventional radial city – readers will be aware, I am sure, that Milton Keynes is built on a grid system – Central Milton Keynes has become all powerful, particularly at the expense of the older towns of Bletchley, Wolverton and Stony Stratford. It is a particular quirk of fate that Bletchley, whose expansion in the years covered by this book began the death knell of commercial activity in the villages, is now itself under the same pressure from Central Milton Keynes.

*Ted Enever – Bletchley, April 2002*

# ACKNOWLEDGEMENTS

In putting this book together I have been overwhelmed by the interest and generosity of all of those with whom I have had contact. At the start of such a project there is always the fear that not enough material will be forthcoming; in this instance, as with 'Cockney Kid and Countrymen,' I need not have worried. At the end of the day it became a question of what had to be left out, not what to include, and if in this context some of my contributors are a little disappointed, then my apologies. To those who have given of their time for interviews and informal chats, and others who have provided photographs, illustrations and text material, I am extremely grateful. They include:

Keith Artingstall, Jock Berry, Jack Bromfield, Bob Brown, Ivern Casey, John and Terry Comerford, Dawn Cousins, Malcolm Deacon, Roly Doggett, Peter Garratt, Denis Gurner, David Higgs, John Jackson, Helen Macario, Ken Meadley, Olive Moser, Bob and Les Page, Guin Parker, Colin Scott, Anna Tagg, Brian Tyers, David Watts, Peter Waylett, Robert Welton, Geoff and Eileen White, Bert Winkfield, Terry Wright and Mary Yates.

I must also extend my thanks to Tracy Whitmore and Zena Flinn, of the Milton Keynes Living Archive, for the supply of and permission to use materials from the Archive's own files; to Sarah Harding, of the Archives and Local Studies Department of the London Borough of Newham; to the staff of the Bedfordshire and Luton Archives and Records Service at County Hall, Bedford; and last but not least, to the staff at Office World in Central Milton Keynes who put much time and effort into copying materials.

Underpinning all those mentioned above are, of course, Paul Bowes and Sally Siddons of my publishers The Book Castle, at Dunstable, and my family and immediate friends who have had to put up with me disappearing at short notice to ferret out some particular fact or photograph. Thank you each and everyone.

'Cockney Kid and Countrymen' I will remember because it was undertaken as a personal millennium project; 'Changing Faces, Changing Places' will be recalled as having been written during the Queen's Golden Jubilee year. Once again, my thanks to all who have made this book possible.

# CHAPTER 1

# NEW BEGINNINGS

I remember the summer of 1945 as halcyon days. In May, six years of war in Europe ended in victory over Nazi Germany and we celebrated with street parties and all sorts of other festivities. A fun fair came to Woburn Sands and set up in the next field to the Recreation Ground, there were garden fetes and concert parties, church and chapel outings. Everyone was in a celebratory mood.

Ordinary life, of course, did not change overnight. The war with Japan, Germany's ally, was still ongoing in the Far East, and at home we still had to contend with rationing, not only for food but for clothes and commodities such as petrol. Still, there was now no blackout, so lights shone after dark from every house window and in spite of history recording the next few years as a period of austerity, there was what we would now call a decidedly 'feel-good' factor emanating from all and sundry. Even school became totally enjoyable!

With many other Aspley Guise children – for I lived in Mount Pleasant – I journeyed every day to Aspley Heath School in Woburn Sands. The school is no longer there but was on the site of what is now sheltered accommodation on the strip of land between the Woburn Road and Sandy Lane. I first went to the school when my parents and I left London after being bombed out on the first night of the London Blitz in 1940. I was a six years-old cockney kid then and as the years passed, the many good friends I made at Aspley Heath School helped in my transformation to a true child of the rural environment. In that summer of 1945 I was rising eleven, had taken and passed the eleven-plus examination which was to give me the opportunity of an education at Bedford Modern School, and was then

1

*Aspley Heath school in the late 1940s. Aspley Court, a development of sheltered housing, now occupies the site.*

thoroughly enjoying those last few weeks at Aspley Heath before my school class became fragmented as many of us went separate ways.

Our class teacher was Mrs Michael and I remember she was keen on country dancing. So those last few weeks saw plenty of activity in that area, as well as other aspects of what I will call 'lighter' education. These included Mrs Michael reading us books such as 'The Water Babies' and 'Black Beauty' and entertainment that we provided ourselves in the form of class concerts, albeit under our teacher's watchful eye. The concerts included individual or groups of children singing, reciting poetry or acting out sketches, and I remember one fascinating afternoon when one of our classmates, a quiet girl called Barbara Summerville, showed us how she kept and bred silkworms. It was also during one of these lighter afternoons that I was given a glimpse of the profession I was to follow – though of course I didn't know that at the time.

In a sketch my friend John Comerford, who lived in Duke Street, Aspley Guise, played the part of a hard-boiled newspaper editor. I had to rush in to his office – a spare desk pulled out in front of the class – saying: 'There's been a big fire in Liverpool!' 'That's not news!' John barked back. 'That happened this morning! I want real news!' I made my exit, to be followed by two more classmates relating news items who were given the same treatment by editor John. One of them, as I recall, was Syd Cox, a big, red-headed bear of a boy who looked somewhat older than his eleven years. Syd, if I remember correctly, lived in one of the cottages at the foot of Aspley Hill, but those cottages have long since gone to be replaced by newer housing. I remember, too, that he had two sisters, Freda, who lost a leg as a small child, and Nellie, the youngest. The family visited Devon on a regular basis, I believe, for Syd would regail the beauties of that county at any opportunity. However, back to the sketch!

After Syd and the other 'reporter' had been dismissed, I rushed in again to tell John: 'There's going to be a murder!' 'Going to be!' said John. 'Now that is news! Where? When?' 'Here and now!' I told him, before using an outstretched right hand as a pretend gun and shooting him on the spot! I must hasten to add, of course, that my future career was not to be that of a murderer but of a journalist and editor. But more of that later.

And so the summer days went on with serious schooling in the mornings, the often lighter approach in the afternoons and the lunchtime break between being even more enjoyable. School lunches were provided by a superb cook named Mrs Burt and taken in Miss Rosie Wells' large classroom for the senior girls which was at the farthest point of the building, close to Sandy Lane. The blackboard behind Miss Wells' desk was used as a menu board and in beautiful copperplate writing – no easy feat using chalk – our fare would be introduced by the words: 'Dinner today'. I think Mrs Burt used to save the entire weekly butter ration for the school for Fridays, for it was then we always enjoyed fish pie, accompanied by a quarter slice of thickly cut bread very liberally spread with the butter. It was delicious.

The lunch break continued with games in the strip of wood opposite school and bordered by the Henry VII Lodge. If some of the girls ventured across the road with us boys we would play hide and seek or tag, but mostly it was just us boys, and the holly saplings we used as pretend swords would be retrieved from the previous day's hiding place, under fallen leaves, before swashbuckling deeds of daring-do filled the next half hour. Our school day started at 9am with a twenty minute break around 10.30am for our free milk. The lunch break lasted from 12.30pm until 1.45pm, then it was back to the classroom, another short break just before three o'clock, and school finished at 3.45pm. Now, it seems, school finishes earlier in the day and I can't ever remember having a day off, as children do now because their teachers are having a training day.

My father, who had been wounded during the war in Italy in 1944, was returned to England earlier in 1945 and was stationed in Yorkshire. He had been home on leave when he and my mother were informed of my passing the eleven-plus and they knew that sometime in July there should be notification of my formal change of schools for the following September. Sure enough, notification came through, but it was not what any of us were expecting.

When my father brought me and mother out of the East End of London's Canning Town in 1940, he did so of his own volition. Being a somewhat independent fellow – to put it mildly – he made it clear he was not going to

4

*An old print of the Henry VII Lodge on the Woburn Road at Woburn Sands, just across the road from the school site. The woods around the lodge were a favourite play area for us children at the school during our lunch-breaks.*

be told where to go by 'some tin-pot clerk at the local council' – as he not very delicately put it. His independence was to have repercussions those five years later for, it transpired, I had never been formally transferred from my London borough's educational records to those of Bedfordshire. Somebody, somewhere, had overlooked me completely because we were not evacuated by the London local authority.

That July notification told us that, far from going to Bedford Modern School as we all hoped and wanted, if I was to make educational progress after passing the eleven-plus, it would have to be at a school back in the East End. It was devastating news.

My mother telegrammed my father immediately and he was given compassionate leave to come home and try and sort out the muddle. What actually happened I never knew, other than that my parents went to Bedford and had one heck of a row with the County education officer. But bureaucracy prevailed, there was no place for me at Bedford or anywhere else locally, so it meant a return to the East End. My halcyon days crumpled into hours of abject misery. What I thought was going to be a wonderful August with lots more celebrations, for the war against Japan had ended with that country's capitulation after the dropping of two atomic bombs on Hiroshima and Nagasaki, now turned into a month of despair as my parents organised living accommodation back in London while I made a round of tearful goodbyes to friends and families.

It is hard to describe the desolation I felt at that time. Coming to the country had been the making of me and I loved the open fields, woods and streams that had become one vast playground for us youngsters during the war years. I had revisited London once during that time, in the late summer of 1944, and although it was exciting to stand outside an Anderson shelter with my grandfather – my mother's Dad – and watch flying bombs buzz overhead, I didn't like the noise and claustrophobic feel of the East End and couldn't wait to get back to Aspley Guise and our own cottage home in Mount Pleasant. Now it was gradually getting through to me that I was to lose all my childhood friends and that the fields, woods and streams were to

*Judy, brought from Yorkshire as a puppy to her new cottage home at 74 Mount Pleasant, Aspley Guise, on a wander down the garden path past my father's greenhouse.*

be replaced by crowds of people, noise and bomb sites.

I knew that at nearly eleven I wasn't a really young child anymore, but even so I cried myself to sleep on more nights than I care to remember. There was just one redeeming factor that made life a little more worthwhile. Judy.

When my father came home on compassionate leave from Yorkshire to try and sort out the educational muddle, he brought mother and me a special gift. He had hardly walked through the door of the cottage before he told us he thought he had something we would both like, but especially me. He undid the top few buttons of his army blouse and from beneath the khaki appeared a fluffy little head with two big brown eyes. It was an eight weeks-old puppy, parentage apparently unknown, but the most adorable little creature you could ever wish to see. Judy, as my father had called her, took to her new home readily and she and I shared many happy times together until she died some eleven years later.

Though Judy brought some better moments to my life during that August, neither she nor anyone else could stop September arriving. For the final couple of days at the beginning of the month when mother and I were at Aspley, I remember trying my luck rabbiting in the fields where they were harvesting, in the hope that I could take my grandparents in London some fresh meat for the pot. But I came home both days empty handed and depressed. On the final evening before we left I walked Judy along Gypsy Lane, the road that joins Mount Pleasant on the Husborne Crawley side of the village, and from beneath one of the big oak trees that bordered the road, picked up two acorns and put then safely in an empty matchbox I found on the grass verge. Those acorns, I resolved, were to be my permanent reminders of life at Aspley Guise. It all seems a little melodramatic now, for what I didn't know, until I got home, was that my parents were to continue renting the cottage so that some weekends we could return. To say I was pleased with that news is an understatement. But I kept the acorns in their matchbox for many, many years.

Canning Town, from where we had been bombed out in 1940, had changed little in the year since I had last seen it and watched the flying bombs overhead.

*Oak trees in Gypsy Lane, Aspley Guise, on a May day in 2002. It was from their forebears, long since felled, that I collected acorns as a keepsake when returning to London in 1945.*

Grandfather's Anderson shelter had gone from his small backyard and in its place flowers grew. Much of the rubble from the years of bomb damage had been carted away too, leaving acres of flat space which made reasonable areas to give little Judy her walks and where I could find the odd clump of groundsel among the sprouting weeds. If I did find any growing it was picked and taken back to grandfather to help feed the half-dozen canaries he kept.

Some buildings remained as visible scars of the war, for if they were damaged but not considered in danger of collapse, they were left alone until decisions were made as to whether they should be demolished or repaired. Canning Town's Trinity Church fell into this category. My mother and father were married there and I was christened there, but only a year or so after the war the site was completely cleared.

I found my new home, part of the top floor of my grandfather's house at 79 Trinity Street, Canning Town, strange, to say the least. We had just two rooms, one which doubled as a kitchen and living room, and a bedroom, which mother and I shared. It seemed to me as if the world had gone full circle, for when we had first moved to Aspley Guise in 1941, after just over a year in lodgings at Woburn Sands, the cottage had no electricity. Now I found that the top floor of grandfather's house was the same, though it did have gas. This meant that if mother baked a cake downstairs in grandma's oven, she could cook by electricity, but if she used the oven upstairs, it had to be gas. Mum soon adapted to these somewhat odd arrangements but I don't think either of us found the lighting provided by a gas mantle over the fireplace very good compared to the electric light that, by then, we had known for some time at Aspley Guise. The thing I missed most, though, was the view from my cottage bedroom window, where I looked across fields to the woods and the tops of the buildings at Woburn Abbey in the distance. Both the kitchen and bedroom windows at 79 Trinity Street looked out on to grandfather's small backyard, which had a corrugated iron fence separating it from a similar backyard and house. Everything was dark and grey. Even when the sun did shine it only made a small patch of light in the backyard; it never actually shone into the house at all.

*Bletchley station just after the war. From here a train to Euston, then the Underground to the Bank followed by a bus journey, took my mother and me back to Canning Town.*

A couple of days after we had arrived and settled in I was hiked off to the Barking Road shops to be kitted out in a uniform for my new school, Plaistow Grammar School, in Prince Regent's Lane, about two miles away. Handing over the appropriate clothing coupons and cash, mother bought me a new pair of short grey trousers – in those days boys seldom wore long trousers until they were about thirteen – a white shirt, grey pullover, navy blue blazer, tie and a navy blue and grey quartered peaked cap. I hated that cap. As a village boy I had gone bareheaded most of the time, resorting only to some scruffy sort of leather flying helmet thing when it was really cold, for mother refused to allow me to wear a knitted balaclava, which many of the other boys sported. To this day I don't know why she didn't like knitted balaclavas. The shiny, very stiff, leather satchel showed the world I was a new boy at Plaistow Grammar and I realise now that the whole ensemble was quite expensive and took a large chunk of the family budget.

So I joined the ranks of first years at my new school, journeying to and from Prince Regent's Lane by trolleybus, a mode of transport my village friends had never seen. My form mistress was a Miss English, a pleasant enough lady who reminded me of a slightly younger version of Mrs Michael and, to my surprise, I found another boy in class with whom I shared the same surname. I don't know why I should have been surprised, because although Enever is uncommon generally – it stems from the Celtic Gweneffre – there are to this day a fair sprinkling of Enevers in London's East End. He and I tried to work out if we were related at all but the best we could come up with was that our grandfathers, or great-grandfathers, might have been cousins.

When I first went to Aspley Heath School in 1940 I found my early London education lagged far behind that of the village children and I struggled with lessons. Now the boot was on the other foot and I was the one in front, thanks to my country schooling. I found myself going over ground in history, geography, English and other subjects that I had been taught by Mrs Michael a year before. Nowhere was this more noticeable than in the basic biology syllabus – which with Mrs Michael fell under the category of nature study – for my new London colleagues had no idea of the migration of birds, the reason leaves changed

*A book of clothing coupons, dated 1945-46. Coupons such as these were handed over for my Plaistow Grammar School uniform.*

colour in autumn and fell off trees, or the life cycle of a frog.

I remember feeling very proud as I explained to the class the intricacies of frogspawn, tadpoles and the resultant frog, all passed on to me at six years old in 1941 by my first country friend, Maurice Circuitt, of Woburn Sands, as well as being covered formally at school with Mrs Michael. At the end of my impromptu lecture Miss English looked at me knowingly and said: 'Excellent. But you've been taught this before, haven't you?' It was obvious you couldn't pull the wool over the eyes of that lady. But what was equally clear was that a London curriculum still lagged behind the provinces when it came to educating its children.

For almost six weeks I stagnated at Plaistow Grammar as I went over familiar ground in almost every lesson. Light relief came in the form of playing on a bombsite opposite, where a couple of rusting cars were bounced on, sat on, climbed in and out of and gradually demolished as 'trophies' were gleaned from any undamaged bits. At the same time I noticed the first prefabricated houses being erected nearby, which quickly became known as 'prefabs' by the local population. Some years later my mother's parents were temporarily rehoused in a prefab after 79 Trinity Street and neighbouring properties were demolished as part of some redevelopment.

During those six weeks my mother and I had managed to get back to Aspley only once, for my mother had found herself a job in Rathbone Street market, serving on the fruit and vegetable stall of two old family friends, Alec and Sarah Thake. Though I didn't feel comfortable with London, and my mother knew I missed the country, I believe she must have felt at home, for it was in Rathbone Street that she and my father had run their own highly successful stall before and during the early days of the war. They specialised in salad produce and the stall was backed up by shop premises nearby.

On that one brief visit to Aspley Guise I saw as many friends as I could, not least my next door neighbour, Alan Ball, who was a little older than me. I remember he and I made plans for carol singing at Christmas, for at least I now knew I would be spending some of my school holidays at the cottage. But unbeknown to me, things were happening which were to turn my life upside down yet again.

*A row of newly erected 'prefabs' on a former bomb site in Blake Street, Canning Town, in 1945.*

During the winter of 1944-45 my grandmother Enever had suffered a severe stroke. She and my grandfather, along with my father's elder brother Jim, his wife and two small children – my cousins – had joined us in Woburn Sands from Canning Town in late 1940. By the mid-1940s, both my grandparents and Uncle Jim's family lived in cottages in The Grove, Woburn Sands, now no longer there as the area forms part of the former Plysu site off Station Road, currently owned by a company called Nampak, who also have a site at Kiln Farm, Milton Keynes.

On the day she was taken ill my grandmother had gone to do some shopping in the Station Stores in Station Road, only a short walk from The Grove and kept at that time by Mr and Mrs Redford. The premises are now used by an interior design business. Gran collapsed in the shop and was taken immediately to Renny Lodge at Newport Pagnell, the nearest thing we had to a local hospital in those days, accompanied by my grandfather who worked in the coal order office of Franklins, luckily sited nearby at Woburn Sands station, the coal being delivered in bulk via the railway sidings which occupied the area where vehicle workshops now stand. After several weeks of treatment she was allowed home but was totally bedridden, having lost completely the use of one side of her body as well as her power of speech.

The family rallied round and my mother and Uncle Jim's wife, Vi, took it in turns to help my grandfather as best they could. When mother took me off to London to go to Plaistow Grammar, it posed a serious problem as to how grandmother could be looked after on a full time basis. There was no National Health Service then and the problem was made worse by her condition deteriorating, as she suffered further strokes soon after we had left. The result was that my father petitioned both the London Borough of West Ham and Beds County Council to reconsider my place of schooling in the light of his mother's illness and the resultant need for my mother to be nearby to help out with her care. Both authorities were sympathetic in the light of the changing circumstances and in late October my parents were informed that I could transfer to Bedford Modern. I was overjoyed. I was going home!

*The Plysu company occupied the site of which The Grove was once part. As the company grew during the 1950s it became Woburn Sands' dominant employer.*

# CHAPTER 2

# THE SCHOOL OF THE BLACK AND RED

The timing of events could not have been better, for half-term at Plaistow Grammar was only a few days away. My Dad obtained further leave, I stopped going to school even before half-term began, and in those few days we had once more left Canning Town with me hoping fervently that, perhaps, this time it was for good. Back in Mount Pleasant I chased around telling anybody who would care to listen that I was back, reintroduced Judy to the smells and vagaries of the allotment path that served the site that ran from Gypsy Lane across the back of the cottages – the allotments are still there today – and began to relish more and more the thought of going to school in Bedford.

A few doors down from us in Mount Pleasant lived Peter Leigh-Lancaster, a quiet, studious boy who was already at Bedford Modern. Peter gave me a brief outline of how the school operated and the routines I could expect. He also recited the words of the school song, which notes its traditional colours, black and red. But some of the things he told me began to take a bit of the gilt off the gingerbread.

It seems there was a thing called 'lock-up' which meant you had to be home and indoors at an early hour every night. That didn't bode well, I thought, for the long summer months when you could be out rabbiting in the cornfields until nine o'clock. And then there was homework, or 'prep', short for preparation, as it was termed at BMS – Peter used the verbal shorthand that pupils used for Bedford Modern School – and there was plenty of it. There was also school on Saturday mornings and in the winter

# THE SCHOOL SONG

When hope is high and our hearts beat strong
And the blood runs warm in our veins;
How we long to race at a swinging pace
In the boat that carries the black and red.
Hold on to the last, 'til the goal is past
In the boat that carries the black and red....

Sons of the spreading eagle crest,
Nurtured here in our homely nest;
'Til the time draws nigh
When we long to fly.
North and south and east and west;
Let us honour the name, let us cherish the fame,
Of the school of the black and red.

*The words of the BMS song which I heard for the first time via Peter Leigh-Lancaster.*

it was compulsory to stay on during Saturday afternoons to watch the home rugby matches of the school first XV. The school was also very strict about the wearing of uniform, he said.

Now although my parents had kitted me out in the Plaistow Grammar uniform, when I went to that school I found I was one of the few boys there who wore the complete outfit. Many of the others had just the blazer and tie, some just a cap, and because of this experience, I suppose, I hadn't given a thought to having to start again with a new uniform. I recall passing on Peter's information to my parents and during the half-term break at BMS my parents took me to the school. There they were interviewed and briefed by the school secretary and the relevant paperwork completed. I came away somewhat chastened and overawed as I realised that this was no Plaistow Grammar and light years away from Aspley Heath. I began to have grave doubts about whether I would enjoy going to a public school.

I think it was the sheer size and presence of the building that first began to worry me. BMS at that time was in the centre of Bedford, two of its four sides facing Harpur Street and Midland Road respectively. Its main, double doors sat at the foot of a castellated tower, and the body of the building on view from Harpur Street carried on the castle-like theme. It all looked very grand indeed, although that facade now merely hides a shopping complex, for the school has long since moved to its present site in Manton Lane.

The entrance used by most pupils in my time, however, was a smaller gate fronting Midland Road and opposite the Woolworth store. This opened into the quadrangle – always referred to as the quad. When we attended that initial interview we went in by this gate and I saw several masters leaving the staff common room and crossing the quad. I remember I gawped somewhat because they were all wearing black gowns.

It transpired that to save my parents the additional cost of a total BMS uniform, I was to be allowed to wear my Plaistow Grammar clothes initially, though with some modifications. I was disappointed at having to wear that horrible cap, albeit with a BMS badge at the front. Not only that, but because I could not swim at the time, on the top and in the centre of the cap would have to be sewn a white shirt button, denoting the fact that I was a non-swimmer. I could only reason that this was because if I ever fell into Bedford's River Ouse, the last thing to go under would be my cap, somebody would see the white button, and hopefully save me! I was later to know boys who went right through their years at school with that shirt button firmly affixed to their little black cap because they had not mastered two lengths of the school baths. I was also told that I needed to wear a County house tie and the school was more than a bit put out when my father dug his heels in about the sort of shirt required. White shirts were the order of the day at BMS, just as they were at Plaistow. But there was a difference. BMS shirts had separate detachable collars, worn with collar studs back and front; my London shirts had collars attached. BMS didn't like that at all; but Dad won the day. My blazer, though dark blue instead of the BMS black, was allowed, with the famous red BMS spread eagle badge to go on the breast pocket.

As I mentioned above, I was to be in County house, the house to which all boys who lived more than three miles from the school were allocated. As BMS drew pupils from all over the county, it was, numerically, a very strong house. North, South, East and West houses catered for boys from those areas of the town and United Boarders – there were three boarding units, Culver, Shakespeare and School – made up the six houses into which the school was divided. There was the usual inter-rivalry, particularly where sport was concerned.

I began my school life at BMS in early November 1945 and felt very uncomfortable. I stood out like a sore thumb in my half-and-half uniform and found that my six weeks at Plaistow Grammar, where I marked time on learning, left me trailing academically. I was put in to the first form, where my form master was a Rev E.J.Bennett. He was also head of what was termed the Lower School, Upper School running from the second year, or form, as it was called, to the sixth form. Perhaps it was my low self-esteem at the time, but it seemed to me that Rev Bennett took a particular delight in throwing up my inadequacies in front of the rest of the class, especially in French dictation where I didn't even have the benefit of a text book to try and follow what was going on.

That first year was a nightmare, both in the classroom and on the sports field where everybody else seemed to have the right gear. They had rugger boots as opposed to my soccer boots, and proper long-trousered cricket whites while I only had short, grey, school trousers. But again, I had a lucky break.

I was one of the youngest in the class and as such could repeat that first year of schooling without it being detrimental later. So I had two years in the first form, and that second time was different again. Now I was one of the pack. I knew my way around school, my early uniform had given way to the correct wear – including those separate collars and a tiny black cap that just perched on the back of your head – I was into all the jargon and style of speech – anything that was good was 'simply wizard' – and I felt comfortable academically and on the sports field.

To get to school we travelled by train on what was known to the various school authorities in Bedford as the Bletchley Line. The pupils who travelled on this route had the reputation of being a somewhat unruly lot, and this applied not only to us BMS boys but to the girls at both the Dame Alice Harpur School and the Bedford High School, as well as the handful of boys at Rushmore School and Bedford School – our arch rivals – and the mixed pupils at the Harpur School.

Peter Leigh Lancaster, Chris Randall, the nephew of the headmistress of what we called the new school in Spinney Lane, Aspley Guise – the old school in Woburn Lane being about to close down – Norman 'Polly' Walsh, who lived in San Remo, Ben Turney and I were among those who caught the motor-train, as it was known, from the halt at Aspley Guise a little after 8am each morning, including Saturdays for morning school. All the halts on the line – Bow Brickhill, Aspley, Stewartby and Kempston – had no proper platforms as they have now. Instead our 'station' was merely railway sleepers laid adjacent to the track and to get up into the train a set of steam driven steps with polished brass handles were lowered by the guard, more often than not a pleasant man named Ken Begley who, when he retired, became landlord of The Old Swan pub in Shenley Road, Bletchley.

Those sleepers served other uses, though, for us youngsters. In the winter their frosted surfaces made an excellent base from which to 'cut out' a slide

*The Bedford-Bletchley motor-train prepares to leave Lidlington station on its journey to Bletchley in 1951. The tank engine pulled the carriages to Bletchley, but pushed them from Bletchley to Bedford. In the centre of the rear carriage can be seen the gap from which the steam steps were lowered at the various villages which had no proper platforms.*

– much to the annoyance of adult travellers such as the Crawley sisters, who lived in a house named Lark Rise, in Gypsy Lane, for quite properly they recognised the dangers – and in summer, with half a dozen textbooks spread across the width of the sleepers to represent a net, the wooden surface doubled as a table-tennis table, the 'bat' usually being a school text book. The complete 'station' complex – sleepers, little waiting hut and the road crossing gates – were watched over by a crossing keeper living in an adjacent house. I believe a crossing keeper still does much the same job now.

Bedford bound pupils were picked up all along the route, from Bletchley and Fenny Stratford, where I remember Peter Morris and the Betteridge brothers, Ron and Tony, lived and where their father, Joe Betteridge, was the well known manager of The County cinema on the Watling Street at Fenny; to Bow Brickhill, where Rosemary and Joe Carter lived at Manor Farm; and Woburn Sands where a whole host of pupils and business travellers virtually filled the train. Among the BMS boys I recall from the slightly later 1940s were Geoff White, John Comerford, John Bowles, Tim Fryer, George Coleman, Keith and Geoff Speed – Keith went on to serve in the Thatcher government of the 1980s and was later knighted – Mick Blofeld and Lawrence White and Ken 'Bunny' Hobbs, the latter two from Woburn. Among the girls I recall were Mick Blofeld's sister Jill, Eileen Woods, Mavis Armstrong, Phyllis 'Pebble' Stone, Enid Phipp, Pat Green, Margaret Mallett, Primrose Emms, Norma Jones and Ursula Adams.

After us at Aspley, Ridgmont saw Peter and Colin Garratt joining the train, along with Tony Parrott and John Inwood and Jean Nicholls from Brogborough. Lidlington, Millbrook and Stewartby added a few more, so that by the time we reached our destination at Bedford St John's station, the train was overflowing. With such a concerted mass of high spirited young people aboard, it was little wonder that at times things did get out of control.

Geoff White, an Aspley boy who was senior to me by several years, recalls the time when somebody – and it was later proved not to be a BMS pupil – unscrewed a light bulb, rammed some silver paper foil from a cigarette packet into the holder, and promptly fused all the lights on the train. It was on the return journey home and in winter, he recalls, because everything was pitch black when all the lights went out. Geoff knew that a couple of compartments along the corridor-style carriage was a group of Dame Alice girls, so he crawled along the corridor on his hands and knees, entered the compartment in the dark and let out a blood curdling yell to frighten the girls. But then the lights came on and Geoff realised he was in the wrong compartment, for he was face to face with a group of local magistrates returning from court at Bedford!

For the train being plunged into darkness that day, every Bedford Modern boy who travelled the route, whether he was on that particular train or not, was caned by our headmaster, me included. Except for Geoff White, who, the headmaster considered, was too senior and too sensible to be involved in such unruly behaviour... The headmaster in question was Rev J.E.Taylor, known to us all as JET, and his stern Victorian values of discipline and punishment meant he ruled the school with an iron fist. He demanded punctuality and if the train was late, such that we were late getting to school, detentions were still handed out despite our protestations. Fellow pupils I have talked to whilst carrying out my research for this book have agreed with me that in all our time at school, we never saw him smile.

All masters at the school were allowed to administer corporal punishment and this 'privilege' was even extended to senior sixth formers who served as monitors, known in other schools as prefects. I remember coming face to face with a monitor, whose surname was Wolf, as I was rushing one day for the afternoon train home. I was chewing a toffee and school rules did not allow eating in the street. The on-the-spot lecture from Wolf – known to his monitor colleagues as 'The Brain' – meant I missed the train and next day I was summoned to the monitors' court where, admitting my guilt, I was caned by a boy perhaps only three years my senior. Oh, the joys of public school... but in later years I realised that it was that sort of incident that taught me self-discipline, perhaps something sadly lacking in so many of today's young people.

But back to Geoff White, whom we all looked up to. Geoff went to BMS the year before me, in 1944, when he was thirteen. The Whites lived on West

*Geoff White and Aspley Guise Cricket Club are synonomous. This photograph shows the side and officials in 1954 and pictured are, back row: Walter Day (umpire) Brian Rice, Terry Comerford, F.A. Dean, E.W. Kitchener, Dr Brian Furber, Cliff Bowler, Stan Whatling (who shared the secretarial duties that season with Stan Brown). Front: John West, J.Sellars senr, Charlie Stone (capt), Eric Delraine, J.Sellars jnr, Roger Thompson.*

Hill, Aspley Guise, and Geoff's father was a skilled carpenter. All who knew Geoff were surprised that he failed the eleven-plus entrance exam for BMS, taken as was mine at a Bedford school. But he says he spent much of the exam period looking out of the window admiring the cars. However, schools at that time were allowed nomination of certain pupils at thirteen and so, two years on, Geoff joined the ranks of the black and red. A gifted sportsman, he soon established himself as a competent rugger player and cricketer and was unexpectedly propelled into the Aspley Guise village cricket team at the age of sixteen.

Returning from Saturday morning school he was met off the train at Woburn Sands by a club official and told: 'You're playing at Luton. Your Dad knows!' and away he went. It was an association with Aspley Guise Cricket Club that continues to this day. At school Geoff went on to play at full-back for the rugby first XV behind scrum-half Dickie Jeeps, who was destined to play for Northampton, captain England and become chairman of the Sports Council. I remember Geoff as always being friendly and helpful, even to us smaller fry, though even he did stray on occasions, for he remembers the way the tip of the monitors' cane went 'ting' as it caught the lightshade on the upstroke before descending...

During his school years I think Geoff was quite a favourite as far as the girls on the train were concerned, though he left after staying on in the sixth form, did his National Service in the Army and then joined the Customs and Excise Service in 1952. It was about this time that one of the Dame Alice girls, Eileen Woods, the daughter of Reg Woods who ran a dairy business in Aspley Hill, Woburn Sands, was dared by a friend to invite Geoff to her school's end-of-term dance.

Geoff says he was met accidently-on-purpose somewhere around the Henry VII lodge area on the Woburn Road and, much to Eileen's surprise, accepted the invitation. Things progressed and though Geoff was posted to Dundee and later Southampton in his career with the Customs and Excise, he and Eileen became an item, to use current language, and were married in 1958. Geoff was a bellringer at St Botolph's at Aspley Guise in his younger

# BLETCHLEY LINERS

Hard winter of youth
Melted into mildness
By hot remembered summers

Hand-slung bunds of snow
Paved a footway
To that open platform
Padded by the cold
The clouded train
Shunted to its meeting place
Of steaming pupils

Sucked them inside
A foggy dankness
Chafed cheeks ran crisp tears
Brushed by unfeeling hands

Chattered exchange
Compared journey's end
And impending early flight
Made companions both
Of child and worker
Soon returned conservatively peered
To pages white and silent
As the window's sliding view

# THE CRICKET CLUB

150 years ago
Life's available space
Allowed a whole cricket week;
Filled summer's content
With pleasure style and grace.
And even when Geoff began
Wasn't leisure still the trend?
Hardly time to score a ton.
Some games started at eleven
Provided he' d prepared the pitch,
Confirmed the match, the umpire,
Arranged the tea, the teams,

Flags out, new bails, new balls,
Umpires' coats –
Six stones each pocket,
Scoreboard up and
One screen –   lime trees end.

Daytime's limit to time spent
On the Common
Less now in two thousand and one.
(Now we're at everybody's beck and call
What with PCs, mobile phones and all)
Village matches condensed to limited overs
And one day Tests till dusk.

But still time to fill the flask
Of memory recall.
'Play' began some time ago.
The only task at all
To get the scorebook up-to-date
Before they bowl last ball!

*Two poems by John Comerford. Bletchley Liners was written for The Eagle, the BMS magazine, but John believes it was not published. The Cricket Club is in praise of Geoff White.*

days and he and Eileen now live in Heath and Reach where they play an active part in the life of their local church, St Leonard's. Geoff has also devoted much time to writing up the history of Aspley Guise Cricket Club. The story covers a period of more than 100 years and John Comerford, who along with Geoff, the late Stanley Brown, Bernard Barnwell and Charlie Stone – 'Pebble's' dad – is regarded as another Aspley Guise cricketing legend, has written the foreword.

John's cricketing ability was quickly recognised at Bedford Modern and he was tutored by 'Fiddy' Rogers, the former Gloucester county cricketer who at that time was our school groundsman. John remembers that Bill Rose, an England rugby trialist, filled a similar role for those pupils who showed talent in this area. John went on to play for the school first XI, captained by R.A.'Gusty' Gale, who went on to play for Middlesex, and for three years the side was unbeaten. Geoff Millman, another member of the team, became Nottinghamshire's captain and England's wicket-keeper, and another lad named Jarret played for Kent alongside Sir Colin Cowdrey. Others went on to play minor counties cricket and to distinguish themselves in games for the armed forces as National Servicemen.

After leaving BMS John played for Bedfordshire and London University, gaining his varsity 'blue' equivalent by scoring 100 against Cambridge University Crusaders. In the same match a young man by the name of Ted Dexter also hit 100. At London University John read Estate Management before going on to gain his Master of Philosophy and an honorary doctorate for his research work. After a busy and rewarding career he now lives in retirement in Sussex where he is a member of the county's Arts Association.

The sporting prowess also extended to John's younger brother Terry who, educated at the Cedars in Leighton Buzzard, won the Victor Ludorum in athletics and was an early member of Ampthill rugby club, founded in 1952.

John and Terry's parents, Bruno and Anne, came to Salford Road, Aspley Guise, with their two children after Bruno was forced out of farm work at Clay Cross, in Derbyshire, by the recession of the mid-1930s. At Clay Cross they lived in the same street as a young man who was to

*A mud-spattered John Comerford comes home in a Bedford Modern School steeplechase in the early 1950s. The races, divided into two junior sections and a senior section, were part of the compulsory sports curriculum for all boys.*

make a name for himself as a parliamentary firebrand – MP Dennis Skinner.

Bruno found a job in a nearby brickyard where he was set to work in the clay-pit. He spent his first day hand-shovelling clay wearing his only suit! He went on to complete 46 years of working life without missing a day and this settled way of life meant the family was able to move to Duke Street, in Aspley, just before the outbreak of the Second World War. It was to be the family home for many years.

The Garratt brothers – Peter the elder, Colin the younger – who lived on a small farm in Ridgmont, can also thank BMS for fostering their love of cricket. Peter, who with his wife Joanna has made 22 Station Road, Woburn Sands, the family home, is a year older than me and admits he found the sporting pressures at BMS hard to cope with. It wasn't that Peter didn't like sport; he just admits that he wasn't good at it. But he followed cricket passionately and soon became involved as a scorer, a task he shared in his later years at BMS for the first XI. Colin was different, and a straight bat seemed to come naturally to him.

By the mid-1950s, when they had both left school, cricket was being played in many local villages though the teams of note were probably Aspley Guise, Great Brickhill, Eversholt and Toddington. In 1957 they decided to try their hands at Eversholt, and Colin soon established himself as a leading player while Peter was seen as a very able administrator. A few years later they were involved in league cricket and their fixtures took them further afield, Eversholt winning the league's Millman competition, named after our BMS colleague mentioned earlier. In 1972 the national village competition was launched and Eversholt, with the Garratt brothers now even more involved, were founder members. Eversholt reached the last 16 in 1973, withdrew a few years later to concentrate on the Bedfordshire league, then re-entered in 1998. In 1999 Eversholt reached the last eight and two years ago, in 2000, lost in the final at Lords to Derbyshire's Alvaston. Colin is now president of Eversholt CC, Peter is chairman, and their respective sons are playing members with Alan, Colin's son, the current captain.

Their association with Eversholt renewed their school acquaintance with

*Terry (left) and John Comerford relax at home with George Battams (right), another Mount Pleasant lad who now lives in Bow Brickhill.*

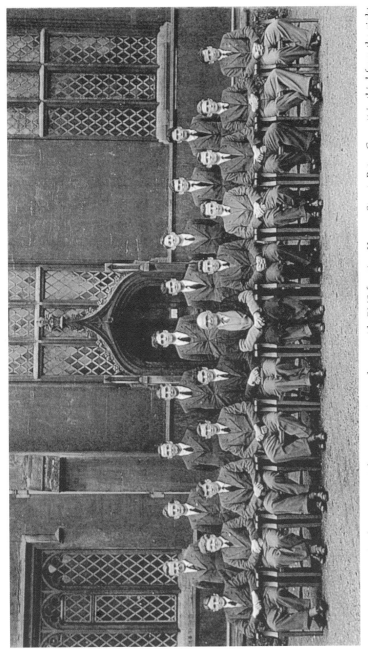

*A formal photograph of Mr P.J. King's house committee taken outside BMS fronting Harpur Street. Peter Garratt is third from the right, front row - the boy on the end is not listed for some reason - and Mick Blofeld, from Woburn Sands, is third from left, front row. Peter Brett, from Eversholt, is pictured third from left, standing, and Bletchley's Pete Morris is third from right, standing.*

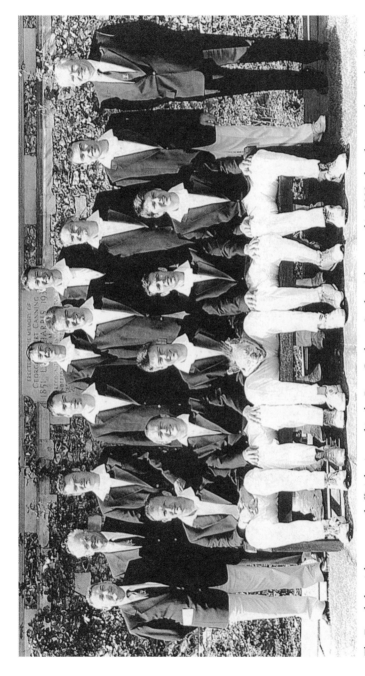

*The Eversholt cricket team and officials pictured in the Rose Garden at Lords cricket ground in 2000 when they were beaten by Alvaston, Derbyshire. Extreme back, left to right: Roger Greenslade, Andrew Litchfield; back row: Mick Humphrey (scorer), Colin Garratt (president), Ron Munro-Hall, Paul Garratt, David Garratt, David Turney, Warren Davies, Peter Garratt (chairman); front: Simon Davis, Peter Morgan, Alan Garratt (capt), Paul Litchfield, Stephen Litchfield.*

another former BMS pupil who lived in the village and was in my form – Peter Brett. The Bretts were a very well known family in the village and I believe Peter's father, Cecil, was the village baker. From his very early days at BMS Peter knew that he wanted to be ordained into the Church and Canon Peter Brett, as he is now, is based in Canterbury.

As the time ticked on at BMS I remember vividly the appalling winter of 1947, one of the worst on record. It began with blizzards in the month of February and on that first day we woke up to find snow two feet deep outside the cottage in Mount Pleasant. Elsewhere in the village high winds had caused drifting and in places the snow lay anything from four to six feet deep.

The whole country ground to a halt – even Buckingham Palace was without electricity and had to be lit by candles. Essential supplies could not get through and we began to experience shortages in the way of bread, milk, meat and above all, coal. All houses then had coal fires – only the homes of better off families had additional central heating systems and these were usually coal-fired – so even keeping warm in the freezing temperatures became very difficult.

It took a great deal of effort to clear the snow around the cottage so that we could move about outside but, on the second or third day, Norman 'Polly' Walsh, Leigh-Lanc – Peter's name was oftened shortened by us in this way – and I decided to try and get to the station to see if we could get to school. As we battled our way through to Aspley Guise Square, unable because of the depth of snow to take our usual short cut to the station across The Close, we met up with Chris Randall. Some of the roads had not even been partially cleared and when the four of us reached St Botolph's church in Salford Road to start the downhill walk to the railway, we found the only way to get there was via a single-file trench cut down the middle of the now invisible road. The snow here was more than four feet deep and as we walked down to the station the only things visible above the sides of the trench were our small black school caps. When we reached the crossing we were told by the crossing keeper to go back home because no trains could get through.

We then set about enjoying our enforced holiday as best we could in the conditions, and for several days enjoyed snowball fights and sledging down San Remo Road or up on Bumstead, a field by the side of West Hill and now home to The Mount development of houses.

Finally the snow cleared but this brought even more problems. The thaw brought floods and the Ouse in Bedford burst its banks. There was four feet of water in the town centre, with swans swimming in and out of the riverbank cinemas. Bedford St John's station was also flooded so again, there was no way we could get to school. When things finally got back to normal we found the amount of 'prep' we had to contend with was phenomenal. But it was the only way we could catch up on lost time and complete that term's academic timetable.

Those winter days at school brought problems even in normal weather. With sport the priority that it was, scheduling regular games sessions for a thousand pupils meant that daylight hours had to be used wisely.

It was in this respect that we would often have lunch, go to the school field for rugger, swimming or cross country running, finish as the light began to fade at about four o'clock, then get back to school for normal lessons which would finish about six. By the time we caught a train, reached Aspley Guise and walked to our homes, we would have been away from the house for close on twelve hours.

I often wonder now what modern educationists and parents would say to that sort of routine for today's youngsters. We walked to and from home to catch the train unaccompanied by any adult and often in the dark on the homeward journey; we faced another walk of a mile or so at the Bedford end and in the morning, getting to school, this part of the trip was undertaken at a breakneck walking pace, because school rules didn't allow us to run, en masse, in the street!

In 1948 Britain was chosen to host the Olympic Games. Dubbed 'the austerity games' because the country was still trying to recover from the effects of the war, life was still difficult in many ways and as such there were no resources to build a purpose built arena. Traditional facilities were used, with Wembley Stadium as the main venue; Henley was used for rowing, Cowes

*Floods in March 1947 in St John's Street, Bedford, the route the Bletchley Liners took to walk to school.*

*The March floodwater in Bedford reached well inland from the river. This shows Midland Road looking towards Silver Street. The tall Elizabethan-type chimneys to the right are those of the BMS building.*

*Looking in the opposite direction to the previous photo – cyclists and cars find the going difficult in Midland Road, close to the All Hallows Lane junction, during the 1947 floods.*

for yachting and Bisley for shooting.

In charge of County house at BMS was Mr P.J.King and 'P.J.' as he was known to everybody, was not only popular with us boys but highly thought of in the world of international athletics. As such he was appointed a field judge at Wembley, officiating in the discus, javelin and hammer events.

The school arranged for various parties of boys to go to Wembley and on the day I was there I was lucky enough to see the Czechoslovakian Emil Zatopek set up a new 10,000 metre record, winning the race by almost a lap. He was an inspiration and cross country running seemed much more enjoyable after that! The games also introduced us to a 30 years-old Dutch housewife and mother, Fanny Blankers-Koen. She won several events and was justly proclaimed the personality of the games.

It was probably about this time that I knew I would never reach the dizzy heights of sporting achievement at BMS, but I did play a fair game of chess. By the next year, 1949, I was in the school chess team – six of us – and we often travelled with the first XV or first XI when we shared a match venue. Match practice consisted of organised sessions at school and plenty of impromptu games played during the lunch breaks taken at County house itself, a large, three storied building in The Crescent, a road roughly halfway between the school buildings and the school playing fields. The playing fields have remained static over the years; the school, though, has moved, so that the fields are now part of the overall site. I remember, too, that on the top two floors of County house were two rooms which housed table-tennis tables, and the rush to get up the stairs for a game, when 'P.J.' declared lunch over, made the stampede at January sales look very tame!

School holidays came and went with our usual out of school pastimes. As we became older, bird-nesting gave way to spending more time playing football or rabbiting – now with the help of a pair of ferrets owned by Lawrence White, from Woburn, and aided and abetted by Ben Turney – or, if it was harvest time, with Judy, the dog, on the edge of the field, waiting to see if a rabbit broke through its first ring of would-be captors. Then there was playing cricket at the bottom of San Remo Road or in The Close, off Bedford Road, where bombs were dropped in 1940. I had my own cricket bat by this time, albeit a cheap and cheerful model, and I remember a gang of us were in The Close early one evening, using my bat. I had to go home early, though I can't recall why, because it wasn't term time so school rules with 'lock-up' didn't apply. Whatever, I left the bat with the rest of the lads to return later, but when it came back via my next door neighbour Alan Ball, it was in two neat pieces, having split clean down the middle! It seemed that John Jackson, Jim Broadbent's step-son who lived in Bedford Road, had given the ball such a crack that my cheap bat just disintegrated. But John had unwittingly done me a favour, for I was able to persuade my parents that I ought to have a proper bat for games at school. In due course I was able to go to 'Fiddy' Rogers at the school field who was able to supply me with a new 'Welsh Wizard' brand bat for £5, a serious sum of money in those days. After not seeing each other for something like fifty years, John and I met up earlier this year to recall the saga of the broken bat and many other memories.

We changed school uniform about this time so that blazers and flannels were worn just for days when we had games. Our new apparel was a rather drab looking grey herring-bone suit, which none of us thought very flattering or glamourous. But as 1949 slipped into 1950, we had other things on our minds. They were the all-important fifth year examinations.

A new examination was to replace the old School Certificate, we learned, and my year were to be the guineapigs. The new exam, called the General Certificate of Education, was to be introduced in 1951. It would comprise two parts, Ordinary level to be taken in the fifth year, Advanced level to be taken in years six or seven. The major difference to us as pupils was that there would no longer be compulsory subjects. For me this meant I dropped maths completely in that fifth year, for although my basic arithmetic was fine, geometry, algebra and further advanced maths were like something from another planet. By dropping maths I was able to spend the scheduled maths periods giving further study to English, history, geography and modern languages.

In those days there was no formal careers guidance on offer though masters did what they could to advise us if we had ideas on what professional or job avenues we might wish to explore. So it was my English teacher, Norman Frost, who asked me to think about journalism as a career.

Norman Frost had taught me a love of the English language and English literature, and I remember feeling flattered when he told me, in what was to be my last year at school, 1951, that it was clear that writing came easily to me. He was sure, he said, that I would enjoy working in journalism and asked me to give the matter some serious thought.

I did as he asked and thought about it a lot, especially on those fine summer Sunday mornings when I would run for several miles, with Judy at my heels, just for the sheer pleasure of it. A favourite route was along Gypsy Lane, into Birchmoor Lane, then cut up into the woods opposite the water works and pumping station, through what we then called Chesnut Grove and then rejoin the road at the junction of Wood Lane and Woodside. Down the hill then to Gypsy Lane and back home via the allotment path. I seldom saw anyone – I was usually up and out by a little after six o'clock – and I was able to ponder quietly on Norman Frost's advice to the rhythm of the run.

He thought journalism allied to me could be an excellent partnership. And, of course, like all good teachers, he was to prove right in the fullness of time.

# CHAPTER 3

# THE WORLD OF WORK

During my time at Bedford Modern School, changes had taken place on the home front. First, in March 1946, during my initial agonising year at BMS, my grandmother Enever died when her condition suddenly worsened.

My father was still serving in the Army at the time but was demobilised soon after, having been warned by a Major Grant Peterkin, an American skin specialist, that his allergic reaction to the new sulphur drugs, with which he had been treated for his wound, could take up to seven years to burn itself out of his system. My father had to keep out of bright sunshine at all costs but as an ordinary working man now employed on building sites this was, of course, difficult. On more than one occasion during those summers after the war he had to take to his bed in a darkened room, his face covered in a mask soaked in calamine lotion with just holes cut for his eyes, nose and mouth. His face and the backs of his hands were swollen, blistered and very painful at these times but Major Peterkin was right; by the early 1950s he could enjoy the sunshine with the rest of us.

When he was demobilised in 1946, Dad insisted that grandfather Enever come and live with us, though in later years I had the impression that the old fellow would have enjoyed his independence by continuing to live in The Grove. But Dad would have none of that, so grandfather duly moved in, we shuffled bedrooms around so that Mum and Dad took the back room, I moved into the front bedroom to share with grandfather and naturally lost my view of the fields towards Woburn! With a two-up, two-down cottage with no indoor water supply, I expect that does not seem a very savoury arrangement given what we enjoy in this day and age. But it was not

*My grandfather, Fred Enever, sawing logs for the fire after he came to live with us at Aspley Guise following the death of my grandmother in March 1946.*

uncommon then for aged parents to move in with their children so that they might be adequately cared for, there being no National Health Service then, for that didn't appear until 1948. With the current state of the National Health Service however, I believe the wheel is beginning to turn full circle, for it seems to me that care from the state is a bit of a lottery and people are more and more having to make personal arrangements, many along the lines I have mentioned above.

Grandfather continued to work at Franklins coal order office at Woburn Sands station and was picked up every morning by one of the Franklins lorries. Towards the end of my school life I would sometimes cadge a lift with grandfather if I knew I could catch a train home that didn't stop at Aspley Guise. My Phillips 'Vox Pupuli' model bike, with its drop handlebars and thin sports tyres, would be put in the back of the lorry and off we would go, the smell of coaldust seemingly everywhere.

During the summer the nicest part of that ride was travelling down Weathercock Lane under the canopy of the tall trees that flank either side of the road. Thankfully, some things haven't changed, for the trees and their canopy are still there today.

I and my classmates sat our 'O' level exams early in June of 1951 and by then I had relayed Mr Frost's thoughts on a possible career in journalism to my parents. My father said he would make sure we obtained copies of the local papers to see if any vacancies were on offer while, exams out of the way, we spent English lessons compiling letters of application to fictitious employers. Then, in the middle of the month, everything seemed to happen so fast.

Dad was working for Newport Pagnell Rural Council at the time and on his travels had picked up a copy of the Bletchley District Gazette. And there, on the situations vacant pages, was what I was looking for; an advertisement calling for a junior to be indentured and trained in journalism. I took the newspaper to school, showed the advert to Norman Frost, compiled my letter of application which he checked and approved, and sent it off.

Within ten days I was called for an interview at the Gazette's tiny office in the premises of Bletchley Printers in Central Gardens Approach, off Bletchley

Road. Bletchley Road is now called Queensway, renamed after a visit to the town by the Queen in 1966, and the old Central Gardens Approach is now part of Prince's Way. The Bletchley Printers building was demolished years ago and the site is now parking space at the back of a video shop.

I found my interviewer a no-nonsense man named Carl Moser, who was the editor. Although he grilled me for the best part of an hour, I thought it went quite well and I liked what was on offer, although I realised it would be hard work. If I got the job, for Mr Moser had shortlisted six of us for interview, I would need to study shorthand and typewriting, elementary law and local government – some aspects of these two subjects being covered by the Gazette's proprietors, Home Counties Newspapers, with classes at Luton – and I would work all day Saturday with a half-day during the week. The indenture period was set for three years, the pay was just over a pound a week to start, with two weeks holiday, and I would be expected to use my own cycle!

The letter saying the job was mine came while there was still two weeks or so to go before term ended. Norman Frost couldn't have been more pleased and I celebrated with a couple of my closest classmates, Bill Wallis and Peter Bywater, both from the Biggleswade area, by having coffee and a cream bun in Pooles Milk Bar next to Bedford bus station, then on its old site not far from the Granada cinema.

I arranged to start work in early August and during the ensuing weeks bought a copy of the Bletchley Gazette to familiarise myself with its style and content. Then, on a warm August Monday morning, two weeks before my seventeenth birthday, I left Mount Pleasant around eight o'clock to cycle the seven or so miles to the Gazette office. I had entered the real world of work, but I will save the description of the daily round of a local newspaper until later.

I use the term 'real world of work' because I was no stranger to going out and earning pocket money. But this was full time work and the start of a career. Towards the end of the war I had gone potato picking on a Husborne Crawley farm to earn a few coppers and as I moved into my teenage years, holiday jobs became the norm.

The first, I recall, was at Frost's nursery, at its site beyond Woburn Sands station. Now the hub of a chain of Garden Centres, the nursery in 1947 was the fledgling business of two men picking up the threads of life after the war. Harvey Frost and Harry Cossom were partners in the business and at that time were concentrating on growing edible crops in the large greenhouses that occupied the site.

My father, who I confess had many jobs locally, for having had his own salad, fruit and veg business prior to the war, he could never seem to settle working for somebody else, gave up his job as a builder's labourer and went to work at the nursery. Here his knowledge of buying and selling in the wholesale markets of London was put to good use by the partners and very soon the firm of Frost and Cossom were making regular deliveries of lettuce, tomatoes and cucumbers, then later a variety of ornamental pot plants, into various outlets in Covent Garden. Len 'Tanner' Britten, who lived with his parents and younger sister, Mary, in San Remo Road, off Mount Pleasant, Aspley Guise, drove the Frost and Cossom vehicle, and with us only a hundred yards away in Mount Pleasant, there were no problems on picking Dad up at something like 3.30am to accompany him if it was thought necessary.

It was in 1948 that I had my summer job there, and it seemed to consist entirely of moving pots of plants from one greenhouse to another or taking the side shoots from tomato plants to ensure all the plant's energy went into developing fruit. Ailsa Craig, I recall, was one of the varieties grown.

Working alongside me was a pleasant lad a little older than me who, it turned out, was Harvey Frost's elder son, Brian. In later years Harvey bought out Harry Cossom to create Frost's as we know it today and, following Harvey's death some years ago, Brian and his brother Adrian took over the business and developed it, very successfully, along the current Garden Centre lines. In the 1960s my father did some contract growing for the company and I know Brian viewed my father with some affection, often describing him to me as 'a real character.'

It was a great shock to the local community when Brian died just before Christmas last year, 2001. I visit the Garden Centre on a regular basis and it doesn't seem the same without him. Brian was often seen on the shop floor,

*The late Brian Frost in a relaxed pose at the Woburn Sands Garden Centre on a warm summer day in the late 1990s.*

*Frost's Garden Centre in its early days and as it began expand.*

*Some of the Selbourne Avenue houses on which I worked in the late 1940s.*

so to speak, chatting to customers, giving advice and having a chuckle or two. I know I am not the only Frost's visitor who misses him.

By the next summer, though, Dad had yet again changed jobs and was back with the bricks and mortar, working for a Bletchley builder, Charles Drabble. Bletchley had begun its rapid expansion, which is examined in Chapter 5, and the Drabble firm were responsible for building the small estate of houses off Westfield Road – what we now know as Birchfield and Ashfield Roads – and the houses that now make up part of Newton Road, Selbourne Avenue and Whiteley Crescent. A coach used to pick up the Drabble workers in Woburn Sands, Aspley Guise and Woburn to take them to the sites, one of the Woburn men being Henry Hobbs, who was a site foreman and father of Ken 'Bunny' Hobbs, one of my Bedford Modern School friends. Ken got his nickname from the fact that he and his father kept and bred show rabbits and when I joined the Drabble band for that particular holiday, I was pleased to see that Ken was already part of the junior workforce.

He and I worked together as a team assisting Andy Armstrong, a Woburn Sands carpenter, whose main task was laying the tongued and grooved floorboards for the upstairs rooms. We had to stack the floorboards up against the outside walls, the tongues all pointing one way, so that Andy could haul them through the window openings and, without any manoevering, drop them quickly into place before tightening them up. When that was done, Ken and I would follow on behind, screwing the boards into the steel joint trusses – those houses are all steel framed – with lengthy screws. Well, that was what the book said, but to screw all those floorboards at four inch intervals with a manual screwdriver – no power 'drivers in those days – would have taken all day, so Ken and I were told to 'screw' them home with a two-pound hammer! I can assure any current residents, however, that the end result was quite satisfactory and I don't think there is any danger of their floorboards giving way! They have, after all, been in place now for well over fifty years.

As the summer holiday of the next year approached, and with Dad now working as a crossing keeper on the railway, Ben Turney, who lived in Mount Pleasant house, opposite San Remo and who was my ferreting tutor, asked if I wanted to join him working for Mr Bill Francis, who farmed at Husborne Crawley. I did, and the first task we were set was to hand-harvest cattle beans – an agricultural form of broad bean – in a field just off the Bedford Road. It was back-breaking work, our hands were cut to pieces and we received a pittance. After a few days we were told by Mr Francis that if we didn't work any harder he would pay by merely giving us the beans we had pulled up! But a bit of Dad's independence must have come rushing through; I'd had enough and I was off.

Within a few days, however, I had managed to find a niche at Mr Jack Green's Hayfield Farm, across the Berry Lane railway crossing at Aspley Guise. Jack's daughter, Pat, went to the Dame Alice Harpur School and the farm had been worked in earlier years by Tim Fryer's family. Tim worked there in the holidays and was the envy of many of us when he reached 16 and used to come to the farm on his BSA 250cc motor-bike with its distinctive royal blue petrol tank. Mick Blofield and Leigh-Lanc were also part of the holiday workforce, as was Shirley Hawkins, a pretty girl who lived with her equally attractive sister, Ruth, and their parents at The Manse, in Salford Road. Shirley, I recall, worked in the dairy but initially Jack Green set me to work in his garden because he had heard, so it seemed, that I had some gardening knowledge and used to spend a lot of time helping my father on the allotments he had taken behind our house.

I remember my first job was to clear and dig over the remnants of an old gravel drive at the front of the farmhouse then dress it out with plenty of farmyard manure – well, there was a lot of that to hand – and once the ground had settled, it was to be planted up with roses. I must have found favour with Mr Green in the way I tackled the task because from then on there was always a job at every holiday. When I finished the drive area I graduated to doing general work about the farm. The winter holiday followed the same pattern of general jobs, the coldest of which was cutting kale for cattle fodder. The kale was four or more feet high and however Tim and I tried, we couldn't keep dry because it always held plenty of moisture on its broad, curly leaves and those droplets went everywhere as we slashed it down with

*Jack Green's daughter Pat, pictured sitting second from right, at a meeting of the Aspley Guise Youth Club. The photograph is believed to have been taken in 1950 after Rev Jefferies, centre, had taken over at St Botolph's, Aspley Guise, from Rev Harry Clothier. Next to him, right, are Les Page and Roger Thompson, with George Battams behind them. Seated at the other side of the table is Colin 'Ginger' Hollis, who lived on West Hill and was proud to become Aspley's first 1950s 'Teddy-boy'! Geoff Hulance is holding up the blackboard demanding subscriptions.*

*A dance at the Social Club, Woburn Sands, in 1950, organised by local hairdresser George Wesley, centre.*

a billhook. But by the start of the following Easter holiday it was rose planting time and back to the drive.

Luckily I knew that roses like to sit in a planting hole with a firm bottom to it, that the graft union between rootstock and flowering stems needed to be at ground level – you can always get that right by laying a short bamboo cane across the top of the planting hole and setting the rose accordingly – and that when you return the excavated earth to the planting hole, a couple of handfuls of bonemeal mixed with it will get the rose off to a good start. Looking back, I enjoyed working at Hayfield Farm during those school holidays but, best of all, that's where I learned to drive a tractor.

It wasn't all work in the holidays though. School rules didn't apply so there were trips to the cinema on Saturday evening via the picture bus run by Leigh-Lancaster's at Woburn Sands and, during the winter months in particular, old tyme dancing was all the vogue and a whole crowd of us went to dances at Woburn, Wavendon, Woburn Sands and Aspley Guise. The Woburn dances, at the Town Hall and with Mr and Mrs Jones from Bletchley as MCs, usually seemed more splendid affairs. The ladies and girls would wear long dresses and the men dinner jackets. We boys just tried to look smart in our suits or sports coats.

It was returning from one of these dances at Wavendon that Bob Page and his sister Betty had a nasty fright. Les, my former cub 'sixer' is their younger brother, and their father, Fred, and mother, Mabel, called 'Auntie Mabel' by just about everyone in Aspley Guise, were very well known. The Page family lived in Bedford Road, just off The Square, and on a pleasant autumn evening Bob and Betty cycled off to Wavendon to the dance. All went well and they had their usual enjoyable evening but it was the return journey home that was to be eventful. Leaving Wavendon close on midnight, they got off their bikes to push them up the incline in that section of Weathercock Lane which has the tall trees and, in summer, the lovely canopy of leaves. On summer evenings it was cool and shady; in autumn and winter it could be dark and eerie, for the street lighting in those days was not of the quality we have now.

'Woodfield' is a house that stands back from the road just where the tall trees start as you travel up Weathercock Lane from the Woburn Sands end.

*Bob Page, right, with his sister Betty and younger brother Les, pictured with their mother, Mabel, just before the war.*

After the war the people who lived in the house petitioned for a reduction in the rates – what we would now call council tax – because, they claimed, the house was haunted. A subsequent tribunal was told that arms appeared out of the walls and all sorts of other ghostly things took place. Well, Bob and Betty had about drawn level with the house when, rolling down the middle of the road toward them was, of all things, a vegetable marrow! Where it came from or who had sent it on its merry way they didn't bother to find out, but it was too close to the so-called haunted house for comfort and to this day Bob reckons they covered that dark bit of Weathercock Lane in record time! The tribunal didn't believe the stories and my theory is that if ghosts existed, they were probably vegetarians...

Bob is a little older than me and entered his world of work in 1943 when he left school at the age of fourteen. His first job was with the well-known Aspley Guise milkman Rupert Ally, where he learned to milk the cows and undertook early morning doorstep deliveries. The worst part of the job, he remembers, was having to walk down the very long drives of some of the bigger houses just to leave a single half-pint bottle. To supplement his wages he hit upon the idea one morning of getting up very early to find mushrooms that he could then sell on the milkround. With a fine basketful of the produce, the dew on them still glistening, Bob knocked on the door of the house next to what was the former Steamer pub, almost next door to Mrs Whitmore's Little Shop, just before reaching The Square. 'Would you like some mushrooms?' he asked the lady of the house. 'Oh, you are a good boy,' she said, taking the basket. 'Thank you so much.' And the door was promptly closed, leaving a crestfallen Bob none the better off and realising that his customer had thought they were a gift!

After a year with Rupert, Bob went on to work at the Zenith electrics factory at Pine Crest, on the outskirts of Woburn Sands on the Cranfield Road, before doing his National Service. He was demobbed in 1950 and a little after went into business as a painter, decorator and general maintenance man with his father, Fred. Bob's father retired in 1974 but Bob kept the business on until 1994 when he retired himself.

*The Steamer pub in Aspley Guise, long before the war. It was from the house next door that Bob Page lost out on his mushroom deal.*

Betty, Bob's sister, left school two years after Bob and became apprenticed as a tailoress in premises that were part of Mount Pleasant House, the home of Ben Turney's family. After a short while the proprietors decided to return to London to carry on the business as, like my own family, they had come to the country early in the war years to escape the bombing. The result was that Betty moved with the firm to Whitechapel where she completed her training. She still lives locally and, like me, enjoys a game of bowls.

Les Page left Aspley Heath school in 1946, just before the school leaving age was raised to fifteen. He remembers the senior boys teacher there, Mr Cooper, as a much respected tutor who was adept at pinging a pupils' ear with his fingers to make sure attention was being paid in lessons. Toward the end of his school days Les arranged to meet one of his cousins but knew that time would be tight if he didn't get out of school promptly at 3.45pm. So the enterprising Les nipped round all the classrooms with clocks, advanced them by a quarter of an hour, and the whole school went home that day at half-past three!

The printing trade was to beckon Les and he joined Fisher's at Woburn, a small jobbing printer where the staff was just himself and Victor Chubb, the general manager. Two years on he 'came home' by joining the Powage Press in Salford Road, Aspley Guise, then owned by Peter Kemp and, at the time, probably Aspley's largest single employer. John Wells, whose family lived in Bedford Road close to the junction with Mount Pleasant, was a fellow apprentice and at lunchtimes all the lads in the firm would play football outside in Salford Road, for there was little motor traffic then. In other quieter moments John and Les indulged in ink pellet fights, the pellets flicked on their way by a printer's steel rule. In one of the storerooms one day, Les waited for John to walk in. He took careful aim as the door opened, the pellet hurtled on its way, and a surprised managing director in the shape of Peter Kemp was duly splattered. Les is still wondering today how he managed to keep his job, but keep it he did, before going on to work for international organisations based at Kings Langley and Watford, eventually returning to work locally at Milton Keynes Web-offset. When that company folded, Les was instrumental in getting the firm of Kestrel Origination off the ground.

*Ladies on a holiday outing in the 1950s from the Powage Press, the printing works in Salford Road, Aspley Guise. Mabel Page is on the extreme right and extreme left is Hilda Peacock, from Husborne Crawley.*

John Jackson, he of the mighty cricket hit and who lived opposite Les, was taken under the wing of Tom Povey, the engineer at the Birchmoor water works in Aspley Guise, on leaving school. For the next six years John was tutored by Tom, who was very well known and lived in Duke Street.

In addition to learning hands-on at Tom's side, John was also able to attend North Beds College of Education on day release. The Birchmoor base was well equipped with a drawing board, instruments and reference books, so John was able to progress quickly. He became known in water engineering circles as 'Povey's boy' and, after his National Service from 1952-54, John joined a small firm of established consulting engineers where, at his interview, the proprietor asked him his full name. 'John Francis Jackson' was the reply. The proprietor looked somewhat taken aback. 'But I thought you were Povey's boy!' he said. Whatever, John added to his learning with many years at the firm, underpinned in the early days with further study at Wolverton Technical College and his qualification as a chartered engineer. He worked all over the world on the setting up, updating and running of water treatment plants before spending the last fifteen years of his working life as a self employed consultant.

John retired some five years ago, now lives in Surrey and, as I mentioned earlier, he and I met up for the first time in something like 52 years in January this year. We talked and talked and could have gone on for three weeks. And there wasn't a cricket bat in sight...

Other boys – and girls – of that late 1940s and 1950s era went, of course, their own different ways. My next door neighbour, Alan Ball, joined the ice cream giants Lyons when they had a base at Bletchley and later moved with the company to Preston, in Lancashire, where he still lives. Malcolm Deacon became a skilled carpenter before diversifying and lives now at Wavendon; his next door neighbour Peter Leigh- Lancaster made the RAF his career and to the best of my knowledge lives in retirement in Australia. Chris Randall has farmed for many years just outside Kettering in Northants while Tim Fryer worked at the agricultural college at Wrest Park, Silsoe, and now has retail premises in Woburn Sands. Ben Turney was with a major agricultural implement supplier, I believe, while Phyllis Stone now lives in South Africa and

*Four of Aspley's attractive young ladies pictured in The Square in the 1950s. Left to right are: Connie Goodfellow, Phyllis Stone, Muriel Lovesey and Mary Britten*

Enid Phipp has a home just outside Bournemouth. Mary Britten worked as a dressmaker in Bedford until she married her late husband, Tony Yates, who was a Mount Pleasant boy. They lived first in Mount Pleasant then moved into San Remo Road, where Mary still lives.

One thing, though, we still have in common. We are now all senior citizens, or old age pensioners if you want to be more blunt, though in each other's eyes I doubt if we appear to have changed much. But of course we have. Our faces have changed, indeed our whole physical appearance has naturally changed, and over the years attitudes change as well. But I am sure I am not the only one of those wartime children and 1950s teenagers who take to heart the words of veteran American entertainer George Burns. 'We all get old,' he once said, 'but you don't have to be old....' Words of wisdom, indeed.

# CHAPTER 4

# GROWING COMMUNITIES

Though history was to record the years immediately after the Second World War as years of austerity, providing new homes to replace those either damaged or destroyed by enemy action was a priority. Alongside this there was a need to build additional homes for a population which was set to expand rapidly as children were born to the families of fathers returning from the war and as growing medical advances saw a lengthening of the natural lifespan.

In Bletchley, as I have mentioned earlier, expansion was already taking place rapidly, and more of that later. In the villages of Aspley Guise and Woburn Sands, growth was more modest, given the amount of building land available, but nevertheless began to be seen by the late 1940s. Burrows Close, tight up but within Aspley's county border with Woburn Sands in Weathercock Lane, was among the first new housing to be seen, where a then new technique of hanging pre-cast shingled slabs on to a steel framework was employed for the outer walls of some of the houses. Within the space of three years or so building was underway at the other end of Aspley, near to the railway line, when farmland off Salford Road became the estate we now know as Trunk Furling. Bungalows were later to be built on the other side of the road opposite Trunk Furlong, between four terraced cottages some four hundred yards from the railway and the cottages adjacent to the line itself. This building then gave an unbroken line of domestic dwellings all the way from the church down the hill on that side. Later the building of the Browns Way development would almost complete an unbroken line on the other side of the road.

In Aspley's Woodside, a local builder, Joe Walker, who had spent much time in Africa, bought a plot of land opposite Woodside Cottage – part of it was the

*A St Botolph's church, Aspley Guise, Christmas party in the late 1940s. Rev Harry Clothier is pictured centre, one row from the back, between the ball and bell decorations. Behind him is Geoff White and, partly hidden by the bell, Bob Brown. Malcolm Deacon is the boy, centre picture, extreme left.*

*An aerial view of Apsley Guise, taken in 1963, when the basis of the village as we know it today was set following post-war building. The ladder-shape of The Mount is towards top right, the triangle of The Square is bottom right and the broad white road centre left is the entrance to the Peers Court development. The old sand pit where we played as children is middle left, just next to the Water Works building.*

*A slightly later dated photograph shows the centre of Aspley Guise more clearly. Many more vehicles are on view and improvements to the rear of the Parish Hall, centre left, can be clearly seen.*

*The Browns Way development in Aspley Guise, built in the field where as children we would dig up clay.*

cottage's vegetable garden which you crossed the road to get to – and Umtali House became the Walker family's home. On the other side of the road and nearer to the walkway linking Woodside to West Hill, a couple of modern Scandinavian type bungalows were put up with a new police house for company. Ten years on and into the early 1960s, The Mount, off West Hill, a select development of detached houses was completed, as was building around the Mentone Avenue area and the grounds of Nether Hill House, the home of musician John Dankworth in the 1950s. Joe Walker, meantime, had moved to a new house at Peers Drive, at the far end of Woburn Lane but then still referred to as School Lane. Other substantial houses were soon built on the site. In San Remo Road, off Mount Pleasant, building was to continue on and off for two more decades though at the time of the first post-war building in the 1960s, the road was still the same as I remembered as a boy – a mixture of stone and rubble as a semi-permanent surface but still with large pockets of loose sand stretching all the way down from its junction with Mount Pleasant to its termination at the gates of Mr Browns's orchard at the bottom.

Robert Welton is the son of Mary and Benjamin Welton – who for some reason was known universally as Fred – and the family, which included two girls, Mary, the eldest of the three and Margaret, lived at number 24, the second house down on the left, In the first house lived Harold Smith, his wife and two children, David and Maureen, and to the best of my knowledge it is still Maureen's home today. Robert was born in 1941 and in the years after the war, particularly the 1947 winter, vividly remembers cars and lorries unable to get back up the unmade San Remo Road in their efforts to rejoin the carriageway proper in Mount Pleasant. The first section of the road adjoining Mount Pleasant dropped very steeply then and quickly became a sheet of ice when any snow or severe frost came.

Ivern Casey, who lived with his parents at 14 San Remo, almost opposite Robert, has similar memories of the snow and ice making the road a nightmare. Ivern, who as a rising four year old met his father at the top of San Remo on his Dad's demobilisation from the army in 1946 with the forceful words: 'I know you; you're my Dad!' recalls a raised manhole cover almost tearing the bottom out of Paddy Geary's black Ford car as it tried to get up the slope. Paddy lived further down the road and was a great man for the greyhounds, taking his own dogs to meetings in the back of the car. If you lived in San Remo and the snow and ice came, the only way to get out with your vehicle was to do what Paddy did; get as far down the road as possible and then take a 30 miles-an-hour run at the slope. Tradesmen attempting to make deliveries found the same problem; getting down was alright, it was getting back that was difficult, though reversing down did save the chore and extra problem in icy weather of just turning round.

By 1952, when Robert was eleven and Ivern ten, social change was well under way. Alongside the desire for better housing was the growing demand for consumer goods of all shapes and sizes. From the early 1950s, washing machines and more efficient vacuum cleaners were becoming a must for most households, closely followed by refrigerators and the need to be on the telephone. In these respects the villages were no different to the rest of the country. Alongside this, more people were beginning to own cars, motorbikes and mopeds so the surfaces of unmade roads like San Remo rapidly deteriorated.

The greater mobility afforded to everyone by car ownership meant that youngsters like Robert and Ivern began to spend more of their social time away from the village. Yes, there was Star Band at Mrs Fowler's Methodist chapel in Mount Pleasant, and two nights a week Mrs Freda Maddy held 'bible search' in her cottage home, also in Mount Pleasant. But whereas those of us only six or seven years older had seldom got farther in our early 'teens than Bletchley for the cinema, a visit governed by the timetable of the Leigh-Lancaster picture bus, youngsters coming toward and into their 'teens could now be taken by family transport to places like the California ballroom at Dunstable.

Robert remembers seeing Joe Brown and the Bruvvers there and the soon-to-be very famous Rolling Stones, with Mick Jagger, when he was a little older. And closer to home, late night dances and concerts at Bletchley's Wilton Hall now became the norm.

Television, too, began to make a great impact in the 1950s and Robert recalls the first set to appear in San Remo going into the home of the family who lived next door, the third house down. It would seem that at the time the technical side of exactly how a picture could be transmitted and received was not that well known to people outside the trade, for Robert recalls one San Remo youngster looking up at the aerial on the roof and complaining that he couldn't see any picture!

In February 1952, a little over fifty years ago as I pen these words, the country learned of the death of the King, George VI. Princess Elizabeth, the elder of his two daughters and on a visit to a game reserve in Kenya when the news broke, was to become Queen. And as I write, we have been mourning the deaths of Princess Margaret, the Queen's younger sister, and Queen Elizabeth, the Queen Mother.

Following the Queen's ascension to the throne there were great celebrations for her coronation in the summer of 1953. The street parties and community events brought reminders of the rejoicing eight years earlier when the war against Germany, and then Japan, had ended. To celebrate the coronation you could buy a pint of beer for what in today's money is 6p; now the average price is £2.50. A loaf of bread was 7p, now around 55p. The average three bedroomed home could be bought for £2,500 – now the same thing averages nearly £100,000. A Morris Minor car cost £358 and though sales were increasing, as I have said earlier, only 14 per cent of all households in the country were car owners. A comparable car today – say a Ford Fiesta – costs anything from £7,000-12,000. When ladies went to the hairdresser a perm cost £2, took five hours, and the dryer was a huge hooded affair. About 90 minutes will see a perm through now – but it will cost around £65.

Other comparisons may well suprise younger generations. Tea was 4p a packet (now £1.75) and cornflakes 7p (£1.25). Cigarettes were 9p (£4.55) and a standard seat at the cinema 8p (£5.50). A bar of chocolate was 2p (34p) and a packet of soap powder 3p (£2.59) which was used, of course, in your £58 washing machine (£500). The television which was installed in the house next door to Robert Welton received only a black and white picture via one channel, BBC, which was only transmitted for five hours during the evening. It probably had only a nine or at most twelve inch screen and cost around £70 compared to today's multi-channel, all-singing, all-dancing, super-digital, remote

71

controlled, wide screen monster at £1,500. A seven inch EP (extended play) vinyl record for your turntable was 30p; today's CD is about £14.

As for computers – well, we hardly knew what they were, with only the most advanced industries using them in their commercial processes and needing acres of space to house them in their massive cabinets. To get some idea of the size of these early machines, visit Bletchley Park one weekend and see a working replica of Colossus, the world's first electronic, programmable computer built there during the war in total secrecy. Some sixteen feet long and eight feet high, the replica was put together by Tony Sale, from Bedford, and other Bletchley Park Trust volunteers. However, rapid technological advances give even today's small personal computers more power and perfomance than Colossus or the commercial models industry could offer in the 1950s.

I would point out, though, one very important point in regard to the price comparisons I have quoted above. Today's average wage is now about £425 a week; in 1952 it was £7.50...

When the Queen's coronation took place in June of 1953 Keith Artingstall was nine years old and had lived in Aspley for only five years. The younger son of Owen and Nellie Artingstall, Keith had an elder brother Neil, nine years his senior, who was a gifted sportsman. The family, who had their roots in the Manchester area, came to Aspley Guise from Blackpool in 1948 where Owen ran a newsagents in partnership with his brother. The family took over premises in The Square formerly run by Mr Tripp and then a Mr Humpley-Gordon, and carried on the established business of newsagents, tobacconists and confectioners. They soon settled into village life and the respect which Owen quickly earned was shown within a few years when he was elected to the Parish Council. As a part sideline to the normal run of business, Owen was a registered agent for Fox's, the turf accountants in Lime Street, Bedford. And I know it was that side of the enterprise that gave my grandfather much pleasure, as he was a man who enjoyed a flutter on the horses! He often used to call me 'Teddy Bear' and always placed his bets under the pseudonym 'Bears' because, he said, I brought him luck!

By 1956, when Neil completed his National Service, Owen had purchased

*Owen Artingstall with, on the left, sons Neil, Keith and wife Nellie, pictured outside their Aspley Guise shop in the late 1940s. The lady with a baby is a relative from Lancashire.*

Telegrams : Shaws, Removers, Blackpool.
'Phone No. 992.

No. AI.213.

27th May, 19 48.

Mr. Artingstall.

Dr. to . . . .

# SHAWS' DEPOSITORY, LTD.

Removal and Storage Contractors,

## WHITEGATE DRIVE, BLACKPOOL.

| | £ | s. | d. |
| --- | --- | --- | --- |
| To removal of furniture and effects from 267 Talbot Road, Blackpool, to The Square, Apsley Guise, Nr. Bletchley. | £25. | 0. | 0. |

Cheques to be made pa...... 's' Depository, Ltd."
Foremen have definite instructions to collect all charges on or before delivery.

*The Artingstall's bill for being moved from Blackpool to Apsley Guise. You got a lot for £25 in 1948!*

74

*The former Post Office building of Miss Alice Holmes which Owen Artingstall planned to run in conjunction with his son Neil.*

the shop premises and house run by Miss Alice Holmes on the other side of The Square. Here it was planned that the family should carry on Miss Holmes' business of chemists sundries and herbalist in addition to retaining the newsagents shop. For just a few short weeks the two businesses were in operation when tragedy struck.

Neil was with his cousin Brian Kittle, who was visiting Aspley Guise, Dave Bodley, a friend from Wavendon and Joyce (Jo) Cook, who lived in Weathercock Lane, Woburn Sands, when the car in which they were travelling crashed on the Stoke Hammond road when returning from Leighton Buzzard. Both Neil and David lost their lives, Jo suffered some injuries and Brian was very lucky to walk away practically unscathed. Both Neil in Aspley, and Dave Bodley in Wavendon, were well known young men and their deaths were a great shock.

I knew Neil, Dave and Jo quite well, the two boys as sportsman and Jo as a fellow student at shorthand classes at Woburn Sands some years before. There was a massive turnout for both funerals.

Owen and Nellie gave up the old Tripp premises shortly after and concentrated their business in Miss Holmes' former premises where they were to remain for many years. In 1967 they had a new house built in the garden fronting the road into which Keith moved when he married Gail Holmes, a Bow Brickhill girl, that year. Owen, a gifted amateur actor, continued to be a stalwart of the local dramatic group, The Chameleons, and in later years enjoyed his game of golf at the Aspley course. Owen and Nellie retired in 1976 and some ten years later, Nellie passed away. Owen died in 1997. Keith now lives in Weathercock Lane, almost opposite Jo Cook's old home, Links View, and for many years has run his own successful hedge cutting and fencing business.

Today, in common with similar communities throughout the country, Aspley Guise is very much a commuter village. Bob Brown, who still lives in the family home on West Hill is, like his father, Stan, before him, very active in village affairs. Stanley Brown was Aspley's parish clerk for many years; Bob has served as a parish councillor since 1960 and since the late 1980s has been the village representative on Mid Beds Council, where he is chairman of the Development Control Committee for the western part of the council's area. Effectively, it is

*The cast of The Chameleons production of 'Home for Good' in the 1960s. Terry Banks is extreme left, Owen Artingstall is centre. Seated is Michael Dexter and right, David Weatherhead. The ladies are Peggy Austin, Marguerite Lewin, Pamela Rutter and Helen Crozier. The producer was Judy Barcham.*

77

Stanley Brown, second from left, is presented with a television set to mark his retirement in 1969 after 44 years as clerk to Aspley Guise Parish Council. Others pictured are, left to right, Stan's son, Bob, Rev A.J.Freeman, Mr Winstanley, Owen Artingstall, Mr Heard, Mrs Blackburn, Mr Rowan Sturdy, Mr Tanner, Mr Harry Armsden.

*The M1 motorway nearing completion just north of Aspley Guise in 1959. The opening of the motorway doubled property values in the village overnight*

Bob's committee that says yes or no to any planning permissions. With this experience Bob is well placed to pinpoint 1959 as being a most crucial year for Aspley Guise, for that was the year the M1 motorway opened. Property values doubled almost overnight, he tells me, and living in the village became an attractive proposition not only for the management and executive staff of Bletchley's burgeoning commercial and industrial base, but for people from the London suburbs and the capital itself. Overnight the M1 had provided a quick and easy way to get both in and out of the capital, for in those days traffic using the motorway was only a fraction of what we see today.

Malcolm Deacon, who lived only a few doors from us in Mount Pleasant, was a carpenter who worked on the building of the local section of the M1. Malcolm was a section leader who, with his various teams, worked anywhere between Watford to the south and Watford Gap to the north, building the necessary forms and shuttering for anything from rain-water gullies to bridges. A keen motor-cyclist – Malcolm used to ferry both my mother and me home from local old-tyme dances on the pillion, but not both at once, I hasten to add – he was given a little BSA Bantam motor-bike to chase up and down the unfinished motorway to check on the progress of his teams.

Malcolm spent five years as an apprentice carpenter, based at Cranfield College, after he left school in 1949. He started work on 3 January, his fifteenth birthday, and when his apprenticeship finished, did his National Service.

He married his wife Pam in June of 1956, three months after leaving the army, but very nearly didn't make it to the altar. Shopping in Luton for the bridesmaids' dresses some six weeks before the big day, Malcolm stopped off to repair a friend's Lambretta scooter.

It seems that the friend had put the wrong amount of oil to petrol in the two-stroke mix and after sorting out the problem, Malcolm took the scooter for a spin around Luton's back streets to make sure it was alright. Everything was going well until he came to a road junction where he had the right of way and began to cross. From out of nowhere came a van which had been modified with windows cut in the back and glazed with ordinary domestic glass.

The van took the front off the Lambretta and Malcolm was catapulted

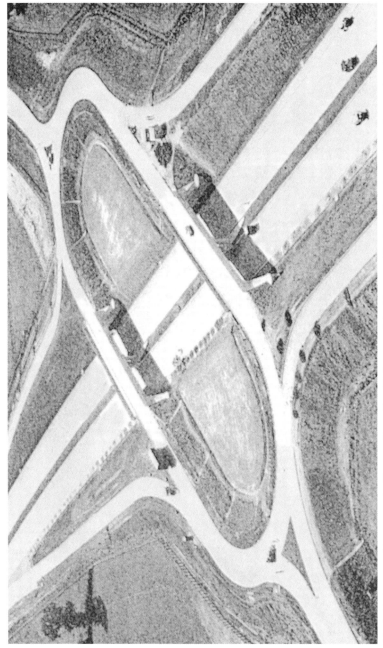

*The M1's Junction 14, serving the Newport Pagnell to Woburn road, looking very bleak and bare just prior to its opening. This was one of the junctions on which Malcolm Deacon worked.*

*The cast of 'Dick Whittington', performed in the late 1940s by the Aspley Guise amateur and juvenile performers, run by Mrs Pirie, at the Parish Hall. Macolm Deacon is the bearded sailor standing, Dorothy Cox is Dick Whittington with Marion Green as the cat at her feet; Phyllis Stone is third from right and Jean Pirie is extreme right.*

headfirst through the windows on both sides of the van, to finish up in a shop doorway with his face and neck very badly cut. He says he came to in Luton and Dunstable hospital three days later with the immortal words: 'Where am I?' He was very lucky to be alive, the gashes on his neck only just missing his jugular vein. But he made it to his wedding; albeit, he says, a little unsteadily.

After the MI opened, Malcolm took a job driving a Marston Valley brick lorry for no other reason, he confides, than wanting to see a bit of Great Britain at somebody else's expense. Ironically, he was one of the first Marston lorries to use the motorway.

By the mid-1960s Aspley Guise was much as we know it today, though some building was taking place at the bottom of San Remo, unmade road or not. Mary Britten, whom I have mentioned on earlier pages, left school in 1946 and after six months at the Plysu factory in Woburn Sands went to work in Bedford as an apprentice dressmaker. After several years in the job Mary left and married Tony Yates in 1953. By 1964, and living with their two young children, Pauline and Douglas, in a small cottage, number 48 Mount Pleasant, the family moved in to one of the new houses being built in San Remo, number 32. Almost immediately plagued by the problems of surface water from the unmade road, Tony and his new next door neighbour, Bill Wilson, who worked in the offices of the brickyard at Brogboro, canvassed all the residents of the road in an attempt to drum up support for moves to get San Remo properly surfaced. In the end they were successful, and San Remo as we know it now was made up after some bad flooding in 1966. Tony went on to help raise money for a swimming pool for the school in Spinney Lane and for many years was a leading light with Aspley's football club. In this role he followed in the footsteps of his father-in-law, Ernie Britten, who with the help of a local businessman, formed the club in 1955.

The focal point of Aspley Guise, The Square, has gradually changed over the years and premises that were once shops are today mostly used as office accommodation. The village still has a Post Office-newsagents and a hairdressers, but like so many other villages, it has lost its commercial heart.

There is one building in The Square that remains dominant, however, and

*Mary Yates (nee Britten) sweeps away flood water in the unmade San Remo Road in the mid-1960s, helped by her two children, Pauline and Douglas with Rusty, the dog. The two children watching are Susan and Trudie, the daughters of Bob and Phyllis Rogers (nee Stone) who lived nearby.*

*Work finally underway and San Remo Road gets a proper surface in 1966.*

*An Aspley Guise football club outing in the 1960s. Norman 'Bunny' Garratt, a Woburn Sands lad, is the first male on the left. The men along the row then are Colin Pursell, Dave Watts, Brian King, Tony Yates and Alan Neale. Mary Yates is third from the right.*

*The Square, Aspley Guise, on a murky day during the very bad winter of 1962-63. The Holt is the large building with the portico, centre.*

*A pre-war picture of Woburn Sands showing The Leys, bottom right, Theydon Avenue, running bottom right to left, and Wood Street, centre. Mr White's nursery is shown, bottom left, and the High Street and Woburn road runs central from the woods, top right. Top left is the edge of Aspley Guise golf course.*

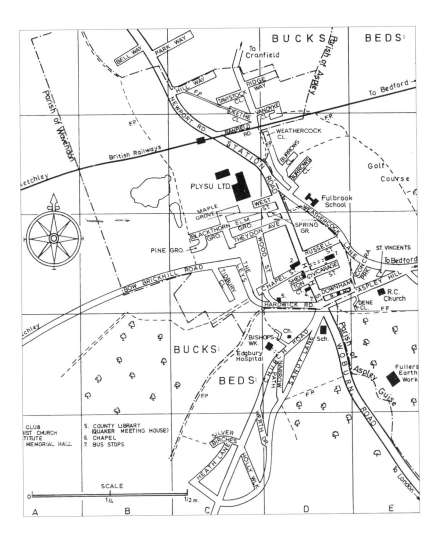

*A map of Woburn Sands in the 1960s shows the framework of the village as it is today.*

89

*Chapel Street, Woburn Sands, just prior to being made up. The new council houses where my Uncle Jim lived, are just out of the picture on the right.*

*Woburn Sands High Street in the early 1960s.*

that is The Holt. The Holt doesn't go by that name today, for it is better known now as Moore Place Hotel, with its excellent restaurant. But to many Aspley residents it will always be The Holt, a building used during the Second World War to house land army girls before being bought in the early 1950s by a man named Fred Wright. Fred and his wife converted the property into an old people's home and for many years Fred and his little red van, taking his elderly residents to church or chapel, were a familiar site in the village. By the late 1960s though, The Holt had changed hands, bought by Len Beswick and transformed into a hotel complete with a cellar bar. It was to be the forerunner of the Moore Place we know today.

Like Aspley Guise, neighbouring Woburn Sands was quick off the starting blocks with its house building soon after the war finished. A village of some 600 people in 1945, new council houses were erected in 1947 in the vicarage field, adjoining Chapel Street and where the former vicar, Rev Shelton, once kept his pony. Among the families to move into these new Chapel Street houses were my Uncle Jim and Aunt Vi with their two young children. They lived at number 36 for many years and their daughter, my cousin Frances, lives there today with her husband, Derek. Aunt and uncle's move came about because the cottages in The Grove, where they had lived throughout most of the war years, were considered then to be below standard, and finally all the properties there were pulled down and the area taken over by Plysu, as I have mentioned earlier.

Chapel Street then was similar to Aspley's San Remo, in that it was an unmade road and used to flood badly, particularly at its bottom end near the junction with Wood Street. But very soon after the new houses went up, the road was properly surfaced, prompting one of the village's Newport Pagnell Rural councillors – Woburn Sands came under this authority's jurisdiction – to seek a change in name. George Wesley, the village hairdresser, was the councillor, and he thought that with a chapel on the corner, the road might be renamed Wesleyan Avenue.... Nothing came of George's attempts and it remains Chapel Street today.

Major building projects followed in Bellway, Blackthorn Grove and Elm Grove, the Blackthorn and Elm site owned by the Austin family, who had a nursery on the site. The Austins bought the nursery after the war from Mr White, who also owned and personally ran the grengrocer's shop in the High Street. This site did pose some building problems, I believe, for I am told there were ponds there big enough to provide some excellent fishing in its earlier days. But to the best of my knowledge there are no drainage problems experienced there today.

Other development came in The Leys and by the late 1950s there was infilling in the unmade roads on the Wavendon side of the station – Hillway and Parkway. Just across the railway line and on the Cranfield Road, Deethe Close had already appeared, named after Deethe Farm half-a-mile further on, and I remember my first friend from when I came to the district in 1940, Maurice Circuitt, and his family moving there.

Another school friend from those years, Douglas Large, lived in the Deethe Close houses, as did one of Uncle Jim's neighbours from The Grove, Joe Williams, with his wife and two sons, Richard and Noel.

By the 1960s the population of Woburn Sands had expanded to some 1500 or more and like Aspley Guise, it was beginning to attract more people from farther afield, thanks to its proximity to the M1. Motor traffic in the area was increasing, noticeably on the 'feed' roads to the M1, and Woburn Sands' Hardwick Road, which marked the county boundary between Beds and Bucks, fell into this category. Where it met The Square the road had no footpath on the Buckinghamshire side as well as turning at quite a sharp angle. Fears were expressed that it was a 'death-trap' corner.

In September 1962 Buckinghamshire County Council began work to widen the road and install a footpath on the Bucks side. First to go were nine lime trees in the garden of Mr Arthur Parker, a well known local businessman and village parish councillor, at 1 Hardwick Road. Mr Parker also lost about fifteen feet of his front garden. Two garages in the car park of The Swan, the large pub on the corner, were also taken down. The road itself was widened by some twelve feet at that point, so that it was no longer a blind corner, and a six feet wide footpath for pedestrians, which extended round to the front of The Swan, was also put in. Other improvements in the form of mini-roundabouts have

*Widening Hardwick Road outside Arthur's Parker's home at number one in September 1962.*

*The landscaped Mowbray Green, Woburn Sands.*

been put in place over the years to improve traffic flow at this point, as well as the removal of the war memorial to its present site outside Shelton Court in 1972. In the late 1960s the double bend at the other end of Hardwick Road where it met the The Leys was realigned by the demolition of Mowbray House and some small cottages. The road here now takes a gentle curve into The Leys and the bulk of the site is nicely landscaped and known as Mowbray Green.

It may well have been Woburn Sands' proximity to the new motorway that prompted Redland Bricks in the early 1960s to apply for permission to reopen the brickworks adjacent to Woburn Sands station. Certainly there was a large residue of clay there and the company put forward a case relating to the need for bricks and the provision of local employment. But people were becoming more environmentally conscious and, having suffered locally for years with the fumes from the brickworks at Brogboro, determined to have none of it.

An informal group of about a dozen local people banded themselves into the Brickworks Protest Committee, chaired by Woburn Sands GP Dr Brian Furber. The committee quickly raised money within the district and asked Mr Desmond Ackner, QC – later to become Lord Ackner – to put its case at a public inquiry into the proposed plans which was held in Woburn Sands from 1-4 June 1965.

Of the two Government Inspectors who took the inquiry, one was from the Alkali Inspectorate. It quickly became clear to local people that this gentleman was far from impartial and was showing favour toward the Redland proposal. An appeal was made against his bias and to formalise local activity, the Woburn Sands Preservation and Protection Society was formed on 10 August under the chairmanship of Dr Jack Kenny.

Dr Kenny, who lived in Woodside, Aspley Guise, and was a senior consultant at Luton and Dunstable Hospital, led the Society into a second inquiry after the complaint against bias was upheld. This second inquiry, held from 26 April-2 May 1966, saw Mr Robin Dunn, QC – a colleague of Mr Ackner whom he recommended – speak on behalf of Newport Pagnell Rural District Council, a raft of Parish Councils and local organisations, and some 1700 local inviduals. The case was so forcibly put and such stringent conditions then imposed on

*Woburn Sands Square in the 1960s, with the war memorial in the centre of the carriageway.*

*The war memorial in its present position adjacent to Shelton Court, an old people's residence in the High Street.*

*The Square in Woburn Sands today, modified to ease the flow of traffic.*

the proposed development that Redland could not comply and the scheme was dropped. The local people had won the day and from then on the Woburn Sands Preservation and Protection Society, though it was to shorten its title later to the Woburn Sands Society, became the environmental watchdog for the area. That responsibility, as well now as many more, remain to this day.

In the twenty or so years from the end of the war to the time of the public inquiries into Redlands proposals to reopen the brickworks, both Aspley Guise and Woburn Sands had grown in population as infilling and the use of farmland for building had brought more homes.

As the places had changed, so had the lives of people living there. In 1945, school for most children meant two round trips a day on foot or at best by bicycle or perhaps a morning trip only on a bus. By 1966 the now familiar 'school run' by car was beginning to make an appearance. Television was overtaking the radio as the favourite media, and in 1966 millions watched as England triumphed to take football's World Cup, albeit mainly on black and white sets. The telephone was affordable and offering everyone instant communication with family, friends and workplaces, whilst waiting in the wings was the transister radio and colour television. In the workplaces modern technology such as electronic typewriters replaced the manual variety and calculators pushed out adding machines. The days of electronic gadgetry gathered pace. By the 1960s the country had entered a phase which the Labour Party's Harold Wilson saw fit to decribe as 'the white heat of a scientific revolution.'

# CHAPTER 5

# BIGGER, BRIGHTER, BETTER

In the mid-nineteenth century Bletchley was no more than a neighbouring village to the prosperous town of Fenny Stratford. But with the coming of the railway in 1838, all that changed, for the line from London to the Midlands was routed so that it passed closer to Bletchley than Fenny. Within a few years Bletchley's station had become Bletchley Junction with the building of the lines to Oxford and Cambridge, and Bletchley's future was assured.

The little village, centred around what we now call Old Bletchley, expanded rapidly with much of the building reaching out toward Fenny Stratford. Before long the two communities had virtually merged and, as the twentieth century dawned, the towns found themselves in a strong strategic position. They were served by one of the country's major roads, the A5 Watling Street, the now main line railway running to the north-west with its varsity towns' branch lines brought increasing prosperity, and they still had use of and access to the canal system with the Grand Union canal. But of the two communities, it was Bletchley that became recognised as the commercial and civic centre of North Bucks.

It was against this background that in 1933 Harold Price and Ron Staniford, two men holding strong Christian views and partners in the firm of Bletchley Printers, decided that Bletchley needed its own newspaper. The area was already served by the North Bucks Times but the partners wanted something more central to Bletchley's ever-growing importance, without neglecting the neighbouring towns and villages. So the first issue of the Bletchley District Gazette came off the presses on 25 November 1933 and, right from the start, the Gazette championed Bletchley's expansion. It was the Gazette that came up with the slogan of a 'bigger, brighter, better Bletchley' and the phrase was quickly taken up by the town council.

In 1934, the year I was born and a year after the Gazette was launched, a 21 years old journalist working for the Banbury Advertiser gave up his job to take on the role of district reporter in Bletchley for the North Bucks Times and Leighton Buzzard Observer. He was Carl Moser.

Born in Manchester, the son of a butler who had an excellent knowledge of fine wines, Carl moved with his family as a child to Lincolnshire before growing up to begin his journalistic career. In Bletchley he was to meet Olive Hankins, a local girl, and they were married in 1937. When war came in 1939, Carl Moser was commissioned into the Royal Artillery and in 1942 was at Singapore when the garrison fell. For the next three years he was a prisoner of the Japanese but somehow managed to keep a detailed shorthand note of everything that went on, which he hid in empty cocoa tins and buried in the camp compound. He was never able to retrieve them.

When he returned to Bletchley in 1946 it was to find that his employers apparently took a dim view of his going off to war and there was no longer a job for him! But Ron Staniford and Harold Price quickly snapped him up to edit the Gazette. He did an excellent job and when Bletchley Printers sold the title to Home Counties Newspapers (HCN) of Luton a few years later, Carl stayed at the helm.

While Carl Moser was incarcerated in a Japanese prisoner-of-war camp, Government eyes in Whitehall were already looking at possible areas for population expansion after the war. In 1944 the Abercrombie report recommended Bletchey as the possible site for a community of some 60,000, news that was music to the ears of Bletchley's Urban District Council. But the plans came to nothing, for more detailed investigation showed that there would be serious problems in the provision of fresh water and the disposal of sewage.

Also in 1944, however, the new Town and Country Planning Act gave local authorities greater powers to acquire land needed for development and the UDC pushed ahead. When the war finished, the Water Eaton and the Trees estates were the first to be built by the Council, chaired at that time by Alf

*Carl Moser, the man who taught me to be a journalist. In the 1970s Carl joined Milton Keynes Development Corporation to handle media enquiries, a role in which I followed him more than a decade later. Carl died suddenly in 1992 while with his wife Olive at a craft fair at Mursley.*

Maycock, a railwayman who lived in Victoria Road. Bletchley's first post-war council house, 167 Water Eaton Road, was opened in June 1946 by the local MP, Aidan Crawley.

In that same year Mr Maycock and his council colleagues found a fight on their hands when Flettons, the brickmakers, put forward plans to extend their local operations. The company wanted to take clay from Loughton, Cold Harbour farm at Shenley, Water Eaton and the area around Skew Bridge, just south of Bletchley. The Council argued that if the plans went ahead in their entirety, they would restrict balanced, normal growth as well as jeopardising any major growth plans that might still be in the Government pipeline. The Flettons proposals, said the Council, would turn Bletchley into a 'brickopolis' and its arguments won the day.

The expansion of Bletchley then began to gather pace and, as I have said in an earlier chapter, I spent a few weeks in 1949 doing my holiday job in the midst of the building. In Westfield Road the gravel pits were filled in and where the library now stands was the site of a large pond with a smaller pond behind it towards Lennox Road and Eaton Avenue. By the turn of the decade, plans were well in hand for massive building in West Bletchley.

But for me the all important morning came in August 1951, when I began work as the Gazette's new junior reporter. I made sure I was there early so by ten minutes to nine I was propping my bike up against the kerb outside the Gazette's Central Gardens office. Somewhat excited, but at the same time apprehensive, I went through the building's front door. There was a little serving counter in the hallway so I gave a knock, because no-one seemed to be about.

I heard some movement in an adjacent office and a man who I learned later was the company secretary to Bletchley Printers, Peter Smith, duly appeared. I explained that I had come to start work, which seemed to throw him somewhat until I explained that it was for the Gazette. He then led me two doors down to the Gazette office, which I recognised because that was where I was interviewed, and it was empty. It was a small, narrow room and against one of the two longer walls was a small desk, which I judged to be where Mr Moser worked, while the other longer wall was taken up by a

*Proudly sporting my National Union of Journalists lapel badge, a photo of yours truly taken by North Bucks Times photographer John Barnes in September 1951.*

*I soon got to know the staff at Bletchley Printers and was fascinated by the sight and sound of printing presses and the dexterous work of the compositors. One of the latter was George Hart, who left to work in Luton in 1953, and spent many years with Home Counties Newspapers at their head office works in that town. George is pictured demonstrating his craft to a group of lady visitors to HCN's premises.*

continuous table top-cum-shelf with three typewriters equally spaced along it. The short wall just inside the door I had entered was home to a large filing cabinet, the far end wall was taken up mostly by a frosted glass window.

I sat there for nearly a quarter of an hour wondering if I had got something terribly wrong. Had I come to the wrong place? Had I got my dates mixed up? Still nobody appeared. Then at nearly ten past nine a tall, slim man who I judged to be around forty, suddenly appeared, looking very surprised to see me. I explained who I was and what I hoped I had come to do, and that was how I met Harold Hepworth, the chief reporter. It turned out that Mr Moser was on holiday, and it had slipped Mr Hepworth's mind that I was due to start. It was very much Mr Moser and Mr Hepworth then and a long time before I got to call the latter 'Heppy', as almost everybody did, and longer still before I was on first name terms with my editor. Then, with a light but quick footstep in the corridor outside, the other member of the editorial staff arrived. She was Margaret Jones.

Margaret, or Maggie as Mr Hepworth sometimes called her, lived in Bletchley and I believe her father was in insurance. She was a couple of years older than me, struck me as being very competent, and although we were never to be the closest of working colleagues, we still got on quite well. In later years Margaret was to make her name as a columnist for both the Daily Express and Daily Mirror, and I saw her last some twenty years ago, in the 1980s, when we met up in London for a lunchtime drink. She was then living in Newport Pagnell.

Somewhat unsure of exactly what to do with me, Heppy sought advice from the editor of what was now the Gazette's sister paper, the North Bucks Times. Like the Gazette, the NBT as it was known, had been bought up by Home Counties Newspapers and had offices at 5 Bletchley Road, almost opposite the entrance to the cattle market. It was edited by a man named Noel Paul, who was to go on to hold a senior post with the Press Council, and he suggested that in Carl Moser's absence I go up to the NBT offices. Off I duly pedalled to report to Mr Paul who then introduced me to Eve Reffold, who wrote the women's column as well as general news, and the two male

*Tom Millligan, the North Bucks Times chief reporter in the 1950s, in pensive mood on an office outing to Clacton.*

reporters, Eric Sadd and Tom Milligan, a tall Glaswegian with the upright posture of a guardsman. Tom had served in one of the tank regiments as a driver during the war and he and I hit it off straight away. He took time out from his routine duties to explain how the two papers worked together.

The Gazette, Tom said, concentrated very much on Bletchley and Fenny Stratford affairs but also took in the neighbouring villages such as Simpson, the Brickhills, Water Eaton, the Shenleys and Loughton, and Drayton Parslow. The North Bucks Times also gave coverage to these areas but extended its range to Woburn Sands, Wavendon, Willen, Woolstone, Stewkley, Mursley and through the Horwoods to Winslow. He showed me how to produce 'copy', the name given to a reporter's typed 'story' – everything was a story, other than little items used to complete a column which were known as 'fillers'. And he explained how, to prevent the two offices duplicating work, nearly all copy was produced with a 'black' – a carbon copy – which the NBT would send down to the Gazette and vice-versa. When I asked did this mean that both newspapers carried exactly the same reports, Tom explained that what you had to do was to rewrite the first couple of paragraphs of say, a Gazette story for the NBT, so that the introduction to the story was different, though the body of the text remained the same.

I was given some menial tasks about the NBT office during the first couple of days, mostly filing cuttings into what was called 'the morgue' – a collection of cuttings from backnumbers of the Gazette and NBT concerning people and places and listed alphabetically so that they could be referred to at any time as background material to current events. Then, by the end of the week, I was put on to 'morning calls' which meant I biked round the town calling on the local clergy, undertakers, the police, council offices and fire station to name but some, just to keep upside of what was going on in the way of accidents, fires, deaths and, on a lighter note, jumble sales, bazaars, general community events and, of course, weddings. The first five days, nipping up and down between the two newspaper offices on my bike, passed quickly and happily enough. I was enjoying every minute of it and took my lunch breaks at the Coffee Tavern by the railway station where you could get a good, strong cup of tea and eat your

*Bletchley's railway station entrance in the 1950s. The Coffee Tavern, where I ate my lunchtime sandwiches, was at the far end of the arched portico. The Post Office vans are parked outside what was then the Bletchley sorting office.*

*A close up of the Bletchley station entrance.*

own sandwiches brought from home.

But then came the acid test. In the course of office conversation I said I enjoyed sport of just about every kind. The diary of events for that weekend was hectic and Bletchley Town were to play a friendly soccer game prior to starting their league programme. I was pushed in at the deep end.

Armed with my notebook and pencil, off I went on the Saturday afternoon. I knew nothing of Bletchley Town football club, other than what I had quickly tried to find out via 'the morgue', and when I returned to the NBT office to write up the game it had to be done in longhand, because I had yet to learn how to use a typewriter – no personal computers with screens then. With the NBT being published earlier in the week than the Gazette, which came out on a Saturday, Mr Paul wanted the match report quickly. As I struggled to get the words down, I could sense his growing frustration as the minutes ticked away.

By the time I had finished and got on my bike to cycle back to Aspley Guise, it was well after six o'clock and I felt shattered. Still, I had written my first report and hopefully it would be published without any heavy editing.

I worried about it all next day, the Sunday, but it went to the back of my mind by Monday morning because I knew Carl Moser was back from holiday, and he was my real boss! But I needn't have worried. The two editors had apparently talked over the weekend when Carl returned to Bletchley, the report was not too bad for a first time effort, and both seemed to think I had the right attitude towards the job.

For much of the rest of the football season I covered the matches of Bletchley Boys Brigade Old Boys. BBOB, as they were known, played on the Albert Street pitch – roughly where the Lidl and Iceland stores are now. Behind the stand and changing rooms was a larger room used as The Barn youth club, run by a Mr Harry Atkins. By the end of the season BBOB had almost adopted me as one of their own and gave me a seat on their committee.

As the weeks lengthened into months my training got under way in ernest and I began classes two evenings a week in shorthand and typing at Aspley Heath School. Via the National Union of Journalists (NUJ) and its training council, I studied elementary law and local government by post and with lectures held on a regular basis at HCN's offices at Luton. Carl Moser was a firm but fair boss, telling and advising on how to handle a story but giving you a right rollicking if you didn't follow his guidelines and didn't produce what he wanted. I went to court with Tom or Heppy to hear various cases involving a variety of charges, the court being held at the police station, close to Fenny Stratford railway station. While the senior reporters sat on the Press bench, I just sat at the back of the courtroom, took notes and listened, so that later I could see how Tom or Heppy handled the case from a reporting view and how this all married in to my studies on elementary law.

It was at court one morning that I met a young fellow just a bit older than me who, sitting at the back of the court as well, seemed to be in a similar situation. It transpired he was James Marchant, whose father, Ernest, was head of the legal firm of Ernest Marchant and Sons. James was there to watch and learn the legal aspects of local court, as against my journalistic side. We were friends for a long time, during which he handled all my legal matters over the years, but sadly James died some years ago.

As we moved into 1952 my daily work pattern began with my bike ride on the morning calls. Anything coming to light here would need following up, particularly funerals and weddings, part of the staple diet of a country newspaper. That, more often than not, took up most of the morning and after lunch there would be 're-writes' or diary events to be covered. In all, Carl Moser made sure I was kept busy.

It was at this time that Bletchley UDC were able to claim back-dated financial support from the Government under the Town Development Act. Suddenly, the Council was awash with money and the plans for even further expansion really took off as the Council brokered a deal with the London County Council to provide homes for what was rather dourly called 'London overspill population'.

A January edition of the Gazette reported that Bletchley would be 'taking part in one of the greatest social experiments of the time, thereby improving the lives of thousands of Londoners while at the same time building up the

*A sea of mud as Bletchley's expansion gets under way to house London's overspill population.*

*The finished product – one of Bletchley's new estates in the late 1950s.*

structure of the town to a size which could provide many more amenities'. Alongside the elected councillors, Bletchley's leading developmental player was the Council's engineer and surveyor, John Smithie, a man of undoubted vision and talent. Under his direction the problems of fresh water supply and sewage treatment were to get sorted out eventually, though I remember going to see him on a totally different matter.

Perhaps it was a combination of my London heritage and love of sport that attracted my to a new form of racing for teenage boys that was sweeping the country at the time. Based mainly in the inner cities which had been badly bombed during the war, the new sport was cycle speedway – exactly the same as speedway proper but with ordinary push-bikes, not motor bikes. The bomb sites of the inner cities provided ideal places to set out an oval track of some 60 – 80 yards in total length, but Bletchley had no bomb sites. Having organised and launched a club – Don Sewell, the owner of a cycle and fishing tackle shop in Bletchley Road was the president and we called ourselves the Fenny Flyers – several of us used to practice in the cinder car park of the Studio cinema. But we needed a proper venue and I found John Smithie both sympathetic and enthusiastic, for he applauded our initiative. He would make some enquiries, he said, but at the end of the day there was nowhere we could call a home. By the time I put on uniform for my National Service in the late autumn of 1952, cycle speedway in Bletchley was a dead duck that never got off the ground.

I remember it was during a quietish news week toward the end of January 1952 that Carl Moser gave me an intriguing little assignment. It seemed that the price of a cup of tea in Bletchley's various cafes differed somewhat and I was charged with cycling round to a variety of places to check on prices and writing a story. The weather was cold and damp, so I started at the Coffee Tavern where I often had my lunch sandwiches and where I knew that railwaymen were charged a slightly lower price than were we ordinary members of the public. Then I went to Norman Green's cafe almost opposite the NBT office, before going to the 46 Cafe on the Watling Street towards Loughton and Healey's cafe in Aylesbury Street, Fenny Stratford. From there I called in at the Pullman cafe by the Brickhill crossroads – a farm shop is on the site now – before making my way home to Aspley Guise. And the first thing my mother said as I opened the door of our cottage was: 'Hello son! Want a cup of tea!'

In late January this year – 2002 – the Milton Keynes Citizen featured my 'cuppa' story in its 'Fifty years ago' column and I wrote to say I remembered it well. In the 1952 Gazette Carl Moser's headline for it was: 'The cup that cheers but does not inebriate.' And the average price for those 1952 cuppas? Just a little over a penny in today's money.

Later in the year the intrepid Mr Moser gave me what I found a somewhat more daunting task. It was a job that gave me an insight into the world of the Women's Institute, usually Margaret Jones' province, for it was she who kept in touch with the various goings on and business of the WI branches in which the Gazette had an interest. But on this occasion it was a group gathering, called a 'Tally-ho' meeting, to be held at Bow Brickhill, and as Margaret, like me, had only a bike to get around on, and Bow Brickhill was on my way home, it seemed logical to Carl Moser that I should be the reporter he sent along. Group meetings, Margaret briefed me, were where representatives from all WI branches in a given area got together to discuss matters of common policy and to review items on the agenda for forthcoming county or national conferences. It was nothing to worry about, she assured me, and there would be tea and cakes and a bit of entertainment.

I cycled off to Bow Brickhill and thought not for the first time that on that route from Aspley Guise to Bletchley, the wind always seemed to blow against you, no matter what direction you were travelling. I reached Bow's Church Hall, made my way up the little steps outside and went in.

I felt immediately that every eye, and of course they were all female and older than me, swivelled in my direction as I stood at the door. The babble of chatter seemed to stop and I could feel myself becoming more than a little embarrassed. I tried to tell myself that this was just another reporting job but it didn't help much; then I was rescued. A petite lady with red hair appeared at my elbow, asked if she could help, and when I explained who I was and what I was there for, promptly found me a convenient seat and brought me a cup of tea and some cake. She continued to put me at my ease so that by the time the business of the meeting began, I felt much better and relaxed. We were then entertained by a lady named Arabella Tulloch who offered a variety of monologues and songs, every one needing a change of costume and rendered in a most theatrical way. Then it was all over and I said my thanks to the lady with red hair, who told me she was a Mrs Whittaker. Five years later, she was my mother-in-law!

It took me some years to realise that the 'cuppa' story and the WI meeting at Bow Brickhill were all part of Carl Moser's training strategy, for he knew that on those sorts of occasions I would have to learn to make myself amenable to different types of people, learn to cope with embarrassing situations and above all, to come away and create a story from what my eyes and ears had gleaned. I have much to thank him for.

Brian Tyers, who lived in Duke Street, Aspley Guise, next door to the Comerfords, began work in Bletchley in 1953. Though expansion of the town was moving apace, the world of banking, he found, was still clinging to its Victorian roots. Brian was a junior clerk at Lloyds Bank where his manager, Mr R. H. Platten was always called 'Sir' by the rest of the staff. Mr Platten owned a car but often came to the office on his bicycle, as did Brian.

Among the six people employed, which included two young, single women, first names were never used and the branch had only a single adding machine which gave a print-out. All the ledgers and statements were written out by hand by the clerks, seated on traditional high stools. Some of the bigger branches did have machines with keyboards on which statements could be produced and Brian learned to use these more sophisticated machines when he attended a six weeks' course at the bank's training centre at Hindhead in Surrey. The course only catered for men, seeing them as potential managers; the girls who went there studied more menial skills, a situation no-one questioned as it was the accepted practice of the time.

In 1955, after I had returned from National Service the year before, John Smithie saw the opening of his brand new sewage works for Bletchley. But with it the works brought a certain hum to the town that had nothing to do with music, and the Gazette carried reports of plagues of flies emanating from the site which were proving more than just a nuisance to householders. Two years later machinery was installed at the works to try and get rid of the smell.

While these problems were going on, though, the house building programme, coupled with the provision of office and industrial facilities, was forging ahead. The Saints estate was quickly followed by the Castles, Rivers and Counties and a whole swathe of what was once open land to the north of Shenley Road had become West Bletchley. On the Watling Street, industrial premises and offices had crept north from the Rodex works on the boundary with Fenny Stratford to reach as far as Denbigh Bridge, though there were social difficulties.

Young local people found themselves often pushed to the back of the queue for council housing. Loosely, the scheme then in operation was that if you came from London and found yourself a job in one of the local factories or businesses, you would be given housing. But if you were a local person and already employed within the town, you had to wait your turn. What didn't help matters was that some newcomers took local jobs to get a house, moved in, then packed in the job to go and work at Vauxhall in Luton or Dunstable where the money was better. For a while there was a grave danger of the 'them and us' syndrome developing and the Council went out of its way to put across the public relations message that both long term residents and newcomers to the community held equal status.

By and large, however, integration between old and new residents did not pose too many problems but I did find myself facing a dilemma in May 1955.

Six months out of the army I found my workload with the Gazette and NBT – now all under the one roof at 5 Bletchley Road, the original NBT office – to be the equivalent of that of a senior reporter. Able to continue my professional studies in the army, and with the added experience of acting as my battalion's public relations officer for the last eight months of my service, I was deemed qualified and at 20 years old classed as an intermediate reporter on intermediate pay, about £5 a week. The rule book said that you did not

*An example of the modern factory development along Denbigh Road in the 1950s. The Wipac factory, which made spark plugs and other motor spares, is the tall building, centre.*

*Bletchley Road (now Queensway) in the late 1950s. The Studio cinema is the white-sided building in the centre. The cinema was demolished some years ago to make way for office development.*

*A busy Bletchley Road in the early 1960s boasting a fine array of shops. For a short while my mother worked in Meyers, the fruiterers and greengrocers.*

*The railway station complex and Old Bletchley from the air in June 1963. Bletchley Road runs from bottom left towards top right and, under the railway bridge, the first turning left is Water Eaton Road. Its small bungalows are now the site of the Cable and Wireless building. In the middle of the picture is Church Green Road running into Rickley Lane. Back towards the bottom of the picture, readers will see there are no buildings along Whalley Drive opposite the curve of Park Gardens. The now demolished 'F' block of Bletchley Park's code-breaking complex, where computers were housed in secret during the war, is shown still standing. The block is the ladder shaped building nearest to Whalley Drive at the bottom right of the picture.*

become a senior reporter until you reached 24, when you came on to senior rates of pay, but here I was – or so I reckoned – doing a senior's job for intermediate money.

I asked Carl Moser if he could do anything about it and, in fairness, he said if it was up to him he would pay me more. But being part of a large corporate organisation, he would have to take my case to head office in Luton. Well, head office was adamant; I was an intermediate, so I was to be paid intermediate money.

For a week or so I chewed over what I might do, one of the options being to go back to Devon, where I was stationed in the army, and take a job with the Express and Echo, the Exeter based evening paper which, as an evening, paid higher rates than weeklies like the Gazette and NBT. I had built up a good rapport with the Express and Echo as the army PR man and they had offered me a job when they knew my service was coming to an end. But some time earlier, while home on leave, I had met Mrs Whittaker's daughter, Barbara, and I knew both she and my mother, particularly, would not want me to disappear again to the West Country.

My Dad solved the problem. He was by now once again self-employed and as well as doing some crop growing and buying and selling a variety of local produce, he was back in the East End of London with his pitch in Rathbone Street, Canning Town, on a couple of days a week. Though he didn't drive himself, Dad had bought an old Fordson van from one of the local milkmen to cart his stuff around and, cash-in-hand and no nonsense, always seemed to find a driver from somewhere. Well, I could drive, and when he said he would pay me £7.50 a week as a permanent driver, I decided to take a chance. It was, after all, half-as-much again as I was getting as a journalist, so I left the bigger, brighter, better Bletchley scene and began to experience getting up at 3.30am and driving to London's Covent Garden and Canning Town. It seemed as if my family heritage wasn't going to let me go.

# CHAPTER 6

# BLETCHLEY REFLECTIONS

Long before Bletchley Council adopted its 'bigger, brighter, better' slogan, the spirit that those words typified was already alive and well in the town. Around 1930, though the world was teetering on the brink of financial depression, Bert Weatherhead, a young Bletchley lad, was convinced that there would still be a continuing demand for radio sets and that the technology of electronics was the way forward. At only 16 years of age, Bert was already capable of building a radio set and, with the help of a slightly older friend, Fred Higgs, he took his first steps into the world of business. Fred was a carpenter who had served his apprenticeship with a firm of local undertakers, Fennemores, for in those days all undertakers made their own wooden coffins. As a skilled man Fred joined forces with Bert to make the wooden cabinets in which all the necessary components, available at the time to construct the set, were housed. One of the first sets produced by the pair was made for a Mr Felce, who lived in Leon Avenue.

At about this time shop premises used as a greengrocer's on the corner of Bedford Street, Bletchley, became vacant and young Bert was encouraged by his mother to set himself up in the shop as a radio specialist. This was duly done and in 1931 the firm of Weatherhead's was established. As well as making purpose-built radios, the premises stocked radios by leading makers – to get the Murphy franchise, much sought after at the time, young Bert had to lie about his years and say he was eighteen, for Murphy would not allow anyone below that age to be one of their agents.

Many radios of the day ran off accumulators and a high tension battery rather than mains electricity, and accumulators needed to be recharged

*The former shop premises of Bert Weatherhead in Queensway, Bletchley, keeps up its tradition of hiring and selling television sets.*

regularly. The norm for a household was to own two, so that one was being recharged while the other was in use. Bert soon built up a useful trade in this area and before long had an established round outside Bletchley, covering many local villages, where the accumulators would be picked up by van one week, then delivered, recharged, the next. The firm charged its customers sixpence (2¹/₂p) for this service! These early radio sets also needed a lengthy aerial to ensure a positive signal and Bert was kept busy running suitable lengths of wire from inside a home to a tall pole at the bottom of the garden where the wire was secured with a porcelain insulator to isolate the aerial from earth.

When war came in 1939 both Bert and Fred saw service in the RAF but quickly settled back into business life after the conflict. Here they put to good use on the home market the technological advances with radio traffic made throughout the war. By the early 1950s Fred Higgs son, David, had joined the rapidly expanding Weatherhead organisation as a technical trainee and by the late 1960s there were nearly a dozen shops stretching across four counties.

David's interest in television was sparked by watching the Burnley-Charlton cup final of 1947 – Charlton won, 1-0 – in a room on the first floor of the Bletchley shop. The place was crowded, Dave remembers, and he peered at the tiny set, sitting with his knees tight up under his chin. He recalls that among his early jobs with the firm was the need to provide television aerials, and that houses in the Husborne Crawley, Ridgmont and Woburn areas, being owned by Bedford Estates, had covenants which did not allow any fixings to the house itself. This meant that the aerial had to be fixed to a larch pole, perhaps thirty feet or more long, which Weatherhead's bought from the Estate's own timber yard at Woburn. Weatherhead's would strip the bark from the larch trunk, treat it with preservative, then erect it in the customer's garden with the distinctive 'H' shaped aerial on the top. And all this to view a single channel – BBC1 as it is now – on a nine-inch set! The cost of providing the aerial was £20 and at £60 or £70 the tiny sets were the equivalent of twelve times an average weekly wage! The van in which they were delivered to the customer's home cost between 300-£400. The fullness of time has seen this situation completely reversed as technology has advanced. The delivery van now costs thousands of pounds, but you can buy a perfectly acceptable colour television for what, perhaps half a weekly wage or even less?

After national service from 1952-54 Dave Higgs progressed to the managerial ladder by the end of that decade and in the 1960s saw the headquarters of the firm relocated to Sandymount, a large house in Woburn Sands High Street. In 1967 he remembers one tricky task undertaken for the late Dorian Williams, the Master of the Whaddon Hunt, who found that a point-to-point race meeting planned at Whaddon coincided with the running of the Grand National at Aintree. Weatherhead's were asked to set up a marquee at the event and provide a bank of televisions so that people could watch the Aintree race. But problems arose at once when it was found that the generators used to provide power upset the quality of the picture, so mains electricity had to be run from a nearby chicken farm. Voltage drops and everything else had to be calculated but, in the end, visitors to the point-to-point were able to watch the race won, by the way, by the 100-1 outsider Foinavon.

In 1971, forty years after he founded the firm, Bert Weatherhead died, but the company was to continue for another thirty years until it closed down in 2001, the last premises to go being the shop at Woburn Sands. Bert's widow, Gladys, switched on the Christmas lights in 2001 at Woburn Sands, where she lives. David Higgs retired from the firm as technical director in 1999; he too lives in Woburn Sands.

Ken Meadley's home at 63 Bletchley Road, (now Queensway) Bletchley, in the late 1940s was one of a terraced row divided in the middle by an alleyway with an ornate arched top. Cut into the brickwork above the arch was a plaque which told the world that this was Rutland Terrace, built in 1882.

The houses, therefore, were a classic example of Bletchley's expansion toward Fenny Stratford after the railway arrived in 1838 and, as a youngster attending Bletchley Road School, Ken used to hurtle up the alleyway at the end of the school day to get home via the back door. Bletchley Road was still then a mix of residential properties and business premises and the residential properties all had sizeable front gardens. A stroll along Bletchley Road at the

*David Higgs, in the light suit, third rank on the right of the picture, on parade with Bletchley Boys Brigade in the 1950s. Ken Meadley was also a staunch member of the Brigade, which was headed by Bletchley Gazette founder Ron Staniford.*

time meant you knew nearly everyone by sight, if not by name, but gradually the houses had compulsory purchase orders put on them as the town's commercial heart was developed. Though the alleyway that Ken ran along as a boy is still there, it now divides Clinton's card shop from the Lloyds TSB building.

School days ended for Ken in the summer of 1953 when he was 15, the same year that Bletchley Road School's well-known headmaster, Ernest 'Barrel' Cook, retired. That September, Ken began work at the East Midlands Electricity Board offices in Victoria Road, Bletchley, as an apprentice electrician, where he worked under the foreman, Fred West, from Bow Brickhill, and where the manager was a somewhat authoritarian man named Sid Blake. Each apprentice then worked with one of the team of electricians at different times so that they obtained the widest possible experience.

Early in his career Ken was working under this system with an electrician named Trevor Felce. Using their normal mode of transport, the bike, they left Victoria Road for Oxford Street, in Bletchley. The working day began at 7.30am and some three hours later Trev told his young companion: 'Come on, lad; time to go up the nob.' So off the two went, on their bikes, to the nob – the Coffee Tavern by the station which I used as a young reporter – where they took a mid-morning break and ordered two teas and two cheese rolls. Only a week before, though, the workforce was told by Sid Blake, in pretty forceful terms, that if anyone was caught leaving a job on which they were working to go off and take a tea break, then that constituted a sackable offence. Still, with a staff of mainly spirited young men, little notice was taken of Sid's warning.

Ken and Trevor had barely settled themselves in the corner seat behind the door of the tavern when in strode Sid Blake – he strode everywhere – closely followed by Fred West. Sid made a beeline for the counter and didn't see Ken and Trevor tucked behind the door. Fred did, but not daring to stop, could merely wave 'get out' signs behind his back! The two left their tea and cheese rolls untouched, dashed outside to their bikes, and made it in double-quick time back to Oxford Street. The irony of it all was that Sid and Fred took up the vacant seats behind the door and Sid apparently remarked on somebody leaving perfectly good tea and cheese rolls!

Day release at technical college formed part of Ken's apprenticeship and he found learning about the theoretical side of things in this way suited him perfectly. After gaining his Ordinary National Certificate and working towards Higher National Certificate, Ken was told he was doing well and was transferred to what was called a student apprenticeship.

This led on to a two year management programme and eventually a degree in electrical engineering. In 1961, though, Ken was an assistant district engineer and by this time a bigger, brighter, better Bletchley was very much a reality. Even the massive west Bletchley estates were virtually complete. Such rapid and vast development did raise problems in the supply of electricity for the area, for up until the 1950s, North Bucks relied on a distribution system that had seen it through the war. In the early 1950s, for example, many of the rural areas had no electric power at all, and for light and heat relied on paraffin and coal.

All that existed in Bletchley was a handful of sub-stations scattered around, such as those at the GPO repeater station, next to the Watling Street bridge over the canal at Fenny Stratford, the one at Water Eaton, and another in the Buckingham Road close to its junction with Shenley Road. The stations were known as 'chapel type' because of their style of design, and so few were they that the engineers could memorise the network. With Bletchley's expansion a new sub-station went in at the Manor Farm estate followed by two more in Whaddon Way and Avon Grove. But even by 1961 the system was only just hanging together. People were complaining of low voltage and the Board was having to juggle all sorts of tasks just to keep the system going. In the main sub-station in Victoria Road, and especially at the time of peak loads in the winter, Vic Firminger, one of the fitters, had to watch the amount of power being used and when it reached certain levels, he was under strict instructions to trip the switch, so cutting off all power to certain parts of the town!

It was clear that major advances were needed to ensure a continuation of supply and the first step was to provide more sub-stations. So the early 1960s saw Ken undertaking a design study of the whole of the western part of Bletchley and initially this took the form of driving slowly around all the new estates in the company Ford Anglia, which he shared with Fred West, and

*The 'chapel type' electricity sub-station. This is the one in Water Eaton, tucked up into a prong of Chestnut Crescent.*

literally counting the number of houses in every street. This allowed Ken to pinpoint exactly where, and how many, new sub-stations should be put in and it resulted in not just one or two, but dozens. Similar surveys in other Board areas, such as Towcester and Wolverton, brought the same results and showed that the load was doubling every eight years as social changes brought more electrical appliances into the home and industry began to rely more and more on electrical power.

The whole of the Board's area was gradually upgraded with new sub-stations and heavier cabling and this work continued until the late 1960s. Then Milton Keynes came off the drawing board to present a different range of problems. From new offices built at Wolverton, a new general manager from Northampton was put in charge with, under him, another senior engineer and three department heads, one for operations and maintenance, one for systems planning and one for construction. Ken was given responsibility for construction, a task he carried through as Milton Keynes developed over the years.

From the utilities point of view, Milton Keynes became the biggest ever single electricity distribution system to be built from scratch in the whole of the country. From what was a fragmented rural power supply came the development of a proper urban system and at one stage the Board was commissioning new sub-stations at the rate of one a week. Ken retired in 1996 and he and his wife Doris are keen bowlers. The secretary of Bletchley St Martin's Bowls Club from 1994 to 2001, Ken then became club president.

Even though Bletchley had made rapid strides in its expansion programme by the mid-1960s, its Urban Council still had three major problems – the disposal of sewage, the disposal of household refuse, and the provision of an adequate water supply. The new sewage works, built on the site of what is now the Tesco distribution depot off Bletcham Way and close to the canal, had the problems of smell which I have alluded to earlier, and very soon was running at full capacity. To try and get rid of the smell, various methods were tried, including spraying the works with deodorant.

Colin Scott, born and bred in Bletchley, was working as a fitter for the Council at the time, though he was to go on to become transport and

*Bletchley's sewage works, isolated by open fields, seen from the air in June 1963. The site is now home to the Tesco distribution depot off Bletcham Way. This photo clearly shows the route of the Grand Union canal alongside Simpson Road with Fenny Stratford bisected by the Bletchley-Bedford railway line.*

cleansing supervisor. Colin tells me the stench was at its worst when the wind was blowing from the east and, living in Simpson Road at the time, he and his neighbours were first in line to receive the offering. Colin was sent to Slough one day to pick up some deodorant and then had to rig up a series of compressors and sprays around the sewage works to push the stuff into the air. All went well until the wind sprang up and the sprays of deodorant drenched the field of corn next door. Within a few weeks straight lines of dead stalks marked where the deodorant had ended up!

As well as the stench problem the works began to overflow as the volume of sewage increased. Just to contain it within the beds the Council built barriers with anything they could find – old machinery, obsolete plant including old dustcarts, and even household refuse. When the Tesco depot was being built a few years ago, Colin went along to see if any of the old vehicles were unearthed. But it appeared that the building line just missed where they were buried so to all intents and purposes, they are still there in the ground. The only thing left as a reminder of the works are one or two of the concrete posts used to marks its boundaries.

To try and dispose of household refuse, dumps were found almost anywhere. A site in Newton Longville was first used, Colin tells me, but this was quickly filled, so the Council turned its attention to Saffron Gardens, the site of an old Manor House and fishponds adjacent to the river and Manor Fields.

When plant began to bury the refuse dumped on the site, it turned up the skeletons of a horse and rider buried in the mud. It was deduced that at some time in history, the pair had found themselves in difficulty on the river bank or in the water and had perished. A sand pit at Little Brickhill was then used as yet another dump and eventually the Council were able to use disused clay-pits at the London Brick Company works in Newton Road.

From a public point of view it was probably the water supply that proved most irksome. Water for the Bletchley area was then drawn from the Sandhouse station at Heath and Reach but in spite of efforts to filter out debris, the supply always contained grains of sand which damaged the pumps that fed the mains. For the local housewives, many now investing in the new twin-tub washing machines, the supply was a nightmare, for clothes that should have come out clean from the machines came out covered in brown streaks. The only way to combat the problem, it was found, was to lay an old towel on top of the machine's load before filling it with water. The towel acted as a filter, caught most of the grains of sand, and the machine produced a clean wash.

In addition to the sand problem there was also concern over just how much water was available for everyone to use. With all the new houses and factories, demand was rising all the time. Under the Watling Street at Fenny Stratford, by the traffic lights at the Aylesbury Street junction, was a large valve which directed flow to various parts of the town. Council workmen were continually having to adjust the valve but one foreman, fed up with the continual adjustments, arbitrarily decided the valve's position and had it concreted in place! Needless to say, this caused more problems and within days the concrete had to be chipped out and the game of half-a-turn one way or another began all over again! Colin left the Council in 1975, is now retired, and lives in South Lawne, Bletchley.

Earlier, in the 1950s and as Bletchley's expansion gathered pace – a situation mirrored in many other parts of the country – the local brickworks increased production to keep up with demand for their product. From Calvert and Newton Longville in the west, right through the Oxford clay belt via Ridgmont, Marston, Stewartby and Kempston Hardwick, the kilns were going night and day.

Jack Bromfield, a Bletchley lad whose father, Arnold, worked in the Bletchley loco sheds after transferring from the railway works at Crewe, found himself caught up in the thick of the brickmaking process during the expansion period.

Jack worked on the railway after leaving school but in 1942, with the war at its height, joined the RAF. Determined to fly, Jack completed his basic and specialist training before being posted to an operational Halifax bomber squadron as a wireless operator-air gunner. He flew missions deep into Germany but on the night of 5 January 1945, his luck ran out, the Halifax was downed and Jack spent the last few months of the war in a prisoner of war camp. When he finally made it back to Bletchley after demobilisation in 1946, he returned to the railway as a signalman at Stoke Hammond. After some three years he took a job as a fork-lift driver in the brickyard kilns at the London Brick Company's Newton Longville works, later transferring to become a lorry driver.

With his eight-wheeler AEC lorry, Jack delivered bricks all over the country. It wasn't long, though, before his administrative ability was recognised and he was promoted to charge-hand in the works. Jack was later called in to the main office and told he was to go on a six weeks' management course at the major works at Stewartby. The course successfully completed, he was to spend many more years at the Newton works as a kiln manager. His responsibilities here were to supervise the running of the kiln, making sure, above all, that there was space inside for the setters and drawers to work unimpeded, and to set the shift patterns for his workforce. With demand for the product ever increasing, Jack saw output at Newton rise to 5 million bricks a week. The major LBC works at Stewartby was producing $14^1/_2$ million a week by this time, Ridgmont – that is to say, the Brogboro' works – and Marston, around 8 – 9 million, and other brickmaking units some 18 million a week. From these figures alone can be gauged the expansion not only of Bletchley, but of the massive building programme going on all over the country.

In 1958 Jack married Ruth Watson, who grew up at Home Farm, now the site of Home Close in West Bletchley, where her father ran the farm as part of the Leon estate. Ruth's grandfather, Jimmy Watson, was enticed from his native Scotland by Sir Herbert Leon to run the farm and assist in the breeding of pedigree bulls. The bulls were shipped out to the Argentine to form the backbone of the vast herds of cattle which helped feed this country during, and immediately after, the war years.

As part of the highly successful and on-going Milton Keynes Living Archive Project, Jack has made an audio tape and CD-ROM of his working life in the brickworks. Both are available to the public and give a fascinating insight into the daily round of an industry that was once one of the district's major employers.

As Bletchley grew and became home to thousands of residential newcomers, so new businesses appeared as well. Not all of them were established ventures that simply relocated to Bletchley; some were home grown and first time efforts. Such was the case with the now established and well known road haulage firm of A.J. Winkfield.

Albert John Winkfield – Bert to his family and friends – was born in July 1930 and grew up in Barking, East London, the son of a haulage contractor. To say Bert grew up with lorries is something of an understatement, for even as a toddler and then a small boy, he was often in the cab of one of his Dad's lorries. When war came in 1939, the then nine years old Bert was shuffled off to Bath in classic evacuee style – gasmask over his shoulder, label pinned to his coat and a bag of goodies in one hand to sustain him throughout the journey. At the Bath end he was duly allocated a place to stay by the billeting officer but for Bert, that city's resplendent Georgian crescents held no magic. He couldn't settle and very soon was back home with the family in Barking. For six weeks during the autumn Blitz of 1940, they virtually lived in the Anderson shelter, the crump of German bombs punctuated now and then by the noise from a lorry-mounted anti-aircraft gun which would stop nearby, fire off a few rounds, and then move on. Statistics now show that in those early years of the war, anti-aircraft fire was not very effective and served more as a morale booster for those on the ground than a deterrent to those in the air.

But enough was enough, and by the end of October 1940 the family were living in the North Bucks town of Olney, close to the Northamptonshire border and famous for its Pancake Day race. Bert went to school in the town before moving on to Wolverton Technical College and, having grown up with commercial transport, knew there was only one place he wanted to be – behind the wheel of a lorry. So, after his National Service in the RAF, he set out to become a driver with the Marston Valley fleet at Brogboro' brick works.

The fleet manager was a Mr P.J. Authors – whose daughter, Betty, was a 'Bletchley liner' at school in Bedford during my time and who subsequently married Brian Harrison of the Woburn Sands removals family – and he told Bert to come back the next year, when he was 21, as company policy decreed this was the minimum age for drivers. Bert did just that and from 1951 spent the next five years doing the same job as Jack Bromfield was doing for London

Brick – taking bricks all over Britain. The Marston Valley lorries, with their distinctive orange livery, were wonderfully maintained, Bert tells me, and the whole Marston operation was highly regarded throughout the haulage industry. Bert drove an Atkinson eight-wheeler, similar to Jack Bromfield's AEC at Newton Longville, and was paid £12.12.6d (£12.62p) for working 66 hours a week. If he had to spend the night away from home he was paid an extra 10s.6d (52$^1$/2p) for the night away.

Around the mid-1950s, British Road Services, the national arm of the haulage industry, was disbanded and its licences made available on purchase to private companies. So in 1956, two years after he married Betty Foulkes, the daughter of Jack and Nellie Foulkes who ran The Plough pub in Bow Brickhill, Bert started up his own business.

He and Betty lived at The Plough at the time and to kick-off the enterprise, Bert used £500 of his own money and a similar sum from his in-laws. His first job as a self-employed man was to deliver steering gear out of Luton to the Morris-Austin car plant in Birmingham, but Bert was soon back among the bricks when work came from his old boss, Mr Authors. Bert remembers the hours were long and the work hard; all the bricks were hand-loaded and if they were drawn from a waiting stack, rather than taken direct from the kiln, then drivers were expected to pitch in and help with the loading. At the other end of the line, the process was reversed, with drivers again helping to unload. Sometimes, though, there was a bonus. If the receiver was short of manpower, the driver would be asked to unload the fifteen tons of bricks on his own, with £1 changing hands, no questions asked...

In 1960, two years after Terrapin joined Bletchley's growing industrial sector, the firm of A.J. Winkfield became its major haulage contractor. It was an association that continues to this day and, at its height, saw Bert running a fleet of ten vehicles. By now, Bert and Betty, with their young daughter Sharon, were living in Bletchley.

Always interested in the history of his industry, and keen on the restoration of commercial vehicles, Bert bought an old Foden lorry some thirty years ago for £160. There was a bird's nest in the fuel tank, the whole

*The Atkinson lorry that Bert Winkfield took over from Taffy Coombes, pictured at the wheel, when he joined Marston Valley.*

*Marston Valley lorries being loaded with bricks drawn straight from the kiln.*

*Bert Winkfield's rebuilt Foden, now the star of many vintage commercial vehicle shows.*

vehicle, such as it was, seemed held together by bits of string, and when you turned the steering wheel, the complete cab moved! The purchase reduced Betty to tears, for, as company secretary responsible for a whole raft of tasks, she thought it a waste of money. But Bert set to work and resolved to give the renovation project some time, however little, every day.

Sometimes, though, this 'little time' would go to the other end of the scale as, after starting work on the Foden in the early evening, Bert would suddenly realise it was four next morning and the milkman was plonking bottles on the front step! But the hard work paid off and the rebuilt Foden has become a star at vintage commercial vehicle rallies throughout the country. Two years ago, in 2000 and at a vehicle meeting held in conjunction with the Tiger Moth rally at Woburn Abbey, the rebuild took the silver cup for best Foden in the show.

Though still putting in a full day's work, Bert has had his son Gary working alongside him for some years, while Betty continues to track down the work and carry out all the office procedures. Successful though he has been, Bert is modest about his own achievements but is quick to praise Betty for her part in the enterprise. 'Without her,' he told me, 'it would never have happened.' For the Winkfields, the impetus of a bigger, brighter, better Bletchley is as relevant today as it's ever been. Though thoughts of celebrations for the company's fifty years in existence may have crossed Betty and Bert's minds, they show no signs of slowing down just yet.

With Jack Bromfield and Bert Winkfield producing and delivering bricks, it fell to Terry Wright to be one of the local men using the product for its ultimate purpose, house building.

Terry was born in Osborne Street, Bletchley, in 1936, and was in the same class as my wife Barbara at Bletchley Road School. Terry's father worked in the building trade in the Kettering area before the war but came to North Bucks to work for one of the major builders in Bletchley, Tranfields. At that time the Tranfield family owned vast tracts of land, both within and immediately outside the town, having recognised the area's potential when they came to Bletchley from Scotland in the 1920s. With the other local building firms of Faulkner, Howard and Ebbs, they became main players in Bletchley's residential building programme.

*A Tranfield gang housebuilding in Bletchley just after the war. Terry Wright's carpenter father is at the top of the scaffolding, extreme right.*

144

During the war new building was put on hold, so for six years Terry's father put away his carpentry tools and worked on the railway. But in 1946 he returned to Tranfields and five years later, when Terry left school in 1951, asked if Terry could be apprenticed with the company. A place was duly found, but only on his father's proviso that father and son didn't work together. It was clear that Wright senior wanted no stigma of favouritism heaped on Terry. So the young apprentice began to learn the bricklaying trade, under the watchful eye of the foreman bricklayer, Harry Sylvester. Though classed as a bricklayer, Terry was to be taught other building skills, such as plastering, and it was at this time that he met Percy Bonner, another bricklayer who, some years later, was to play a major part in the rebuilding of my April Cottage home at Bow Brickhill, covered in my next chapter.

On his first morning Terry was put to work on a house in Buckingham Road, opposite Tattenhoe Lane. The building was already up to roof height and Terry realised there was some ladder climbing to do, though no-one had thought to ask him if he had ever been up a long ladder before! But he managed it and was later to work on sites in Church Green Road and on houses and bungalows in Shenley Road around the Craigmore Avenue area. In 1956 he went into the Army to do his National Service and the indication of the somewhat slower pace of life in those days may be judged by the fact that, when he returned to work for Tranfields in 1958, he had only missed out on about a dozen houses being built in Shenley Road!

It was about this time, Terry tells me, that he noticed things beginning to change in the industry. Charlie Drabble's firm were once more very much on the Bletchley building scene after their initial success with the Westfield Road and Selbourne Avenue pressed steel housing projects, which I mentioned in Chapter 3. The firm had obtained contracts from the local authority to build the large estates we now know as West Bletchley, the provision of these estates made possible by the Council using compulsory purchase orders to acquire much of the Tranfield-owned land.

However, part of the deal allowed the smaller, local builders to have some input and in the case of Tranfields, who employed at that time perhaps twenty or thirty men, this meant splitting the workforce so that half the men worked on Council building, while the other half carried on with private work. Harry Sylvester looked after the private gang while John Meager, who lived in Buckingham Road, was foreman for the Council squad.

By now, building firms began the move toward lessening their direct labour force in favour of sub-contracting to self-employed tradesmen and labourers. Dudley Tranfield, then head of the family firm, began to suffer from poor health and took the decision to follow this employment route with the company. He told his employees that he would effectively wind-up the firm but he still wanted to design and build houses, so if they wanted to go self-employed, he would employ them as his builders. John Meager approached Terry to see if he would join up with him and together they forged a good working partnership, building Tranfield designed houses all the way down Shenley Road toward what is now Standing Way, including the house Terry now lives in with his wife, Eileen, whom he married in 1960. From there the workforce moved to sites in Newton Longville and, all told, Terry and John worked together for almost twenty years. In later life they were to renew their partnership as fellow members of Bletchley St Martin's Bowls Club.

Terry decided to strike out on his own around this time because, he says, he was seeing builders who were not builders making money. He has retired now after creating a successful business but still looks back on his apprenticeship days with great affection.

Like all youngsters he had his leg pulled by the 'old-stagers' of his day, such as the time he was sent to Street's, a little shop on the corner of Park Street, in Bletchley, to get the proverbial pint of pigeon's milk. The lady in the shop took pity on him. 'I think they're having you on, my duck,' she told him. 'But I can help you out!' She gave him a very small bottle of milk and told him to tell his tormentors that it was all the pigeon's milk he could get hold of. Terry handed it over in such a way that his site colleagues knew they had been rumbled.

Another youngster on the firm was not so lucky. Told to go to Cleavers, the builders' merchants with premises on the corner of Water Eaton Road, now the site of the Cable and Wireless building, the lad duly presented himself

*Terry Wright at work on a Church Green Road site when a young apprentice in the early 1950s. In 1952 and 1953 Terry took the building industry's award for the best bricklaying apprentice in Bucks. A certificate and new trowel and hammer were awarded to mark his achievements.*

at the counter and asked for a long weight to be debited to Mr Tranfield's account. He was told to sit down until he was attended to. Two hours later the lad was getting agitated and asked how much longer would it take to be served. The counter clerk looked at his watch and told him: 'Well, you've had your long wait; off you go!'

# CHAPTER 7

# BOW BRICKHILL

In 1955 I soon settled into the routine of early mornings and driving to Covent Garden for Dad. And I confess I saw the place properly for the first time. As a very small child I would regularly accompany my father on his trips there, perched up beside him on the high seat of his horse and cart, then to be carried around the place either on his shoulders or tucked under his arm. But now I was seeing it as an adult and understanding what was going on as my father did his buying and the produce was delivered by the market's porters to the van.

At that time Convent Garden was at its traditional site just off London's Strand, for it was to move to its present location at Nine Elms, south of the Thames, in the late 1970s. I don't know if it is the same now, but certainly forty or more years ago, many people were under the impression that to buy goods in Covent Garden, you went to an auction. Nothing was further from the truth. In both the main and ancillary areas of the market, produce was displayed within open fronted shop-like premises or in areas or bays marked off by chain-link panels. Salesman were on hand and after examining the goods a potential buyer queried the price. Given that, some haggling usually went on until a deal was struck or the buyer decided against a purchase. If you bought the goods you were given a sales invoice which you took to the firm's cashier desk. The invoice showed the goods you had bought at so much a box, bag or case, plus a porterage fee to cover delivery to your vehicle. As a buyer, you then moved on to another firm for a different range of goods, for just like an ordinary High Street, not every Covent Garden merchant offered the same sort of produce for sale. Some specialised in imported fruit – oranges, grapes,

*The former milk-float Fordson van in which I drove my father to Covent Garden in 1955. As I built up my village fruit and veg deliveries, the Fordson was replaced by a series of Bedford vans, culminating in the early 1960s with a purpose-built mobile shop body on a Bedford chassis.*

150

lemons, bananas – others concentrated purely on home grown vegetables – potatoes, carrots, cabbage, peas and beans. But whatever you needed, you would find it in Covent Garden, and virtually at any time of the year.

The buying and selling process had its own jargon and, to some extent, code of conduct. With the jargon, if you asked a vegetable salesman how much were his cauliflowers, he knew you were a rank novice straight away, and a couple of coppers would be mentally added to his price before you were told what it was. The reason was that no-one in the capital's vegetable wholesale markets, whether it was Covent Garden, Stratford, Spitalfields or the Borough, would ever refer to cauliflowers by that name. In market terms they are 'heads' and are usually packed in dozens, 18s or 24s. So the normal approach to a salesman would be: 'What price your 18 heads, old son?' and, hopefully, you would be in business. Similarly. apples, oranges and peaches would always be initially queried by count – how much your 126 Kent Cox's if apple buying, for example – and varieties of potatoes were always sold by name.

Tomatoes were bought by grades – pink and whites being the half-dozen to the pound size, with twelve pounds being packed to a box or tray. Imperial weights were always used, for not until 1973 was decimal coinage introduced, followed by measures in metres and weights in kilos. Pink and white crosses were slightly smaller tomatoes in size, whites were very small – what we would now call cherry tomatoes – pinks and blues were larger with the latter slightly mishapen. On the code of conduct side, no salesman worth his salt would ever sell you goods knowing that they were of an inferior quality to what he said. If they had been damaged in transit, or were of a variety that didn't 'travel well' as it was termed, he would tell you so, then if you bought something in that latter category, you knew that they needed to be sold quickly from a retail point of view. Sometimes the odd slip- up would occur; a case of oranges, perhaps, would seem perfect when opened, but half way down would contain a larger than average proportion of bruised or mildewed fruit. A word with the salesman next time round would usually get you a credit note without any hassle, and buyers didn't take advantage in those situations. Reputation in Covent Garden at that time meant a lot, and I have no reason to believe it has altered over the years. So all in all I think I learned quite quickly at my father's elbow, for he was much respected. But, at the time, I was just the driver. He was the skilled buyer.

On the days when I didn't need to drive Dad to London I was given other jobs to do, such as collecting produce from local growers or farms ready for transporting to London on the next trip. My father always tried to make sure that you didn't run a vehicle empty, because if you did, it wasn't paying its way. And on the afternoons I had off following early morning trips, I kept my hand in at writing by ferreting out stories and sending them either to the local papers or, if they might be little items of general interest from, say, one of the local councils, then getting them off to the London evening papers.

Within a few months, and at my Dad's suggestion, I began to use those afternoons in another way, as well as still managing to write during the evenings. I began to build up a retail delivery round in Aspley and the neighbouring villages.

After a year Dad and I had a routine in place whereby I now had set days to take him to London – Saturday was one – but on the other days I would load up the van and go round the villages selling fruit and veg direct to customers at their door. The earnings began to mount up nicely and Dad and I came to an agreement that for the use of the van on some days I would now drive him for free, while everything I made from the round would be mine. I began buying my own produce in Covent Garden, using my own cash, and with a little bit of freelance money from journalism coming in as well, Barbara – who was a hairdresser at Phyllis Cooper's Aylesbury Street, Fenny Stratford, salon – and I were able to get married in 1957.

The two years since I had left the Bletchley Gazette had not been all work, work, work, for I had taken my interest in music a little further by joining forces with half-a-dozen other fellows to play at local dances, birthday parties and other functions. Dave Higgs, mentioned in the previous chapter, was on piano, Don Bell, then manager at the Bedford Arms Hotel at Woburn, the hotel being one of my customers, was on string bass and was very experienced, having played with the legendary Joe Loss Orchestra for many years, and

*A young man and his music. Dave Higgs on piano, Denis Borley on guitar and myself on drums at my 21st birthday party held at The Bell, Aspley Guise, in August 1955. The young lady in the picture is Mary King, who lived in Hardwick Road, Woburn Sands, and was herself an accomplished pianist.*

Dennis Borley, whose wife Grace worked in the Gazette office, played guitar. The 'front line' as it's known among musicians, was made up of Terry 'Satchmo' Barfield, a young Bletchley lad from Saffron Street, on trumpet, Pete Jackson, from Newport Pagnell, on clarinet, and Jimmy Ruff, from a Hanslope farming family, on trombone. I was the drummer and sometimes we would be augmented by other local musicians. We had some great times, played in concert at the Granada cinema at Bedford in front of 2000 people, and generally enjoyed ourselves. We tended to view rock-and roll, introduced a few years earlier by Bill Haley and his Comets, as 'commercial tripe' and played a hybrid jazz with a rhythm section admiring the modern school, while the front line was out and out traditional. Still, it seemed to work, and at times we played just for the beer and sandwiches. I sometimes wonder what might have happened to us musically had we changed our outlook on 'commercial tripe' – but that was then and we played what we wanted to play for the enjoyment of it, not the financial considerations.

Barbara and I were married at All Saints church, Bow Brickhill, on 5 January 1957. We came out of church under an archway of trumpets and drumsticks and the reception at the Bedford Arms went well. Don Bell did three jobs that day – my best man, in charge of the hotel and playing in the group for dancing at the reception. What we didn't bargain on was most of the musicians in North Bucks deciding to wander in at some point in the afternoon and at certain times the Bedford Arms dining room was host to a full 14 piece dance orchestra. Everyone joined in the dancing, even the hotel staff!

While mentioning the Bedford Arms I cannot pass without reference to Bernard Dooley, who was barman there for many years. Bernard's home was in Brooklands Road, Bletchley, but he lived-in at the hotel. In winter he used to build superb fires in the bar's hearth, made up of what regular users of the place called 'Bernard balls' – ovals of solid fuel carefully placed one on top of the other. Bernard was a man of small stature, mostly easy going, and probably then in his fifties. The hotel was then owned by Trust House Forte and in recognition of his many years service, Bernard was given a substantial block of the company's shares. Sunday lunchtime was a get-together time for us

*January 1957 and Barbara and I leave All Saints church, Bow Brickhill, under an archway of trumpets and drumsticks. On the left, nearest camera, is Terry Barfield, with Dave Higgs and John Comerford. On the right, nearest camera, is Mike Waldron, then Peter Hartley and Denis Borley.*

regulars and on one occasion a man and his wife stopped off for drinks and coco-colas for their children. The Bedford Arms stocked only pepsi-colas, so Bernard poured out a couple to complete the order.

The man became somewhat abusive, saying that pepsis were not what he had ordered, and did not give Bernard time to explain that the hotel only carried that brand. The fellow went on and on and as he did so, Bernard picked up his cloth and began to polish an empty glass. We knew what was coming as the polishing became more and more energetic; it was a sign that easy-going Bernard was getting riled. 'I'll have you know I'm a share holder in this company!' the man finally roared. Bernard stopped polishing suddenly, put the glass down and put his elbows on the counter. 'Are you now', he said, looking up at the man. 'Well, so am I! How many have you got?' It stopped the man dead in his tracks and off he went.

The first home that Barbara and I had at Bow Brickhill was a small cottage in London Lane, left to Barbara by her grandma Whittaker and next door to George and Ivy Whittaker, my new in-laws. After my jazz-drummer hero Gene Krupa, we named the cottage with his surname, painted the front door bright yellow to give it a modern look, and settled in to life with Barbara working in Fenny while I continued with the fruit and veg round and whatever I could do in the way of freelancing.

I found living in the village very pleasant. I soon made many friends, not least of them the rector of All Saints, the Rev Ronald Groves-Brooks. Donald Gilks, Barbara's cousin who lived in a council house in Bow's Station Road, became a Friday night beer-and-skittles partner, Fred West helped us out with additional electrics when we first moved in to the cottage – and advised us to hire our cooker from the Electricity Board, which we did for one shilling and sixpence a week ($7^{1}/_{2}$p) – and I already knew Joe Carter and his sister Rosemary from our school days in Bedford. To top it all, mother-in-law's wedding present to me was a German Shepherd puppy whom I named Riff, after the Stan Kenton jazz classic, Intermission Riff, and he and I spent hours in Brickhill woods which were only a hundred yards from our front door.

At this time, the late 1950s, Bow still had a thriving farming heart. Four

*Our first home in London End Lane, Bow Brickhill, which we called 'Krupa' after a jazz drummer, as it is today.*

*The Rev Ronald Groves-Brooks with the all-female All Saints church choir in 1951. Left to right, back row, are: Barbara Whittaker, Shirley Parker, Joy Daniels, Rosemary Clarke, May Beckett, Sylvia Guess. Front row, left to right: Rosemary Carter, Rev Groves-Brooks, Lita Guess.*

*Barbara and I, with Riff growing up fast, pictured in the summer of 1957 on the allotment path behind the Mount Pleasant cottage where I grew up.*

farms – Tilbrook, run by Don Burgess; Poplars with John Colgrove, Manor Farm, with Joe Carter senior, and Rectory Farm, where Jean Over lived with her family, were all viable agricultural units. The village was well served by a post office, run by Mrs Lizzie West but which for many years previously was the province of Maudie Collins, who was awarded the MBE for her long length of service, and there were two other shops, the one on the sharp corner to Woburn Sands run by Katie Clinch, the other, The Pines, a little further up the hill and almost opposite the Church Hall, owned by the Misses Frost, Maggie and Thurza. Mobile traders appeared on a regular basis – Bernard Langler, the baker, from Great Brickhill, Mr Hurst, the fishmonger from Fenny Stratford, the Co-op butcher's van with Albert Metcalfe in charge, the Co-op milkman, Ben Wright, and both Janet Hill from Fenny and me with fruit and veg.

That mainstay of village life for many years, paraffin, was brought round by Percy Collins, one of twin sons of Maudie Collins, the other being Dennis, who lived away. Maudie lived a long life and when I first met Percy, he was the paraffin man, village taxi driver and, most importantly, the village postman. You could almost set your watch by Percy's morning delivery – eight o'clock for our part of the hill – and the bane of Percy's life was the growing use of mail shots for advertising, particularly by the soap powder manufacturers. 'Damned Daz', Percy would complain to anyone in earshot. 'Bagfull of it; damned Daz!'

What one of his regular taxi customers would make of such grumbling, we could only guess, for Rev Groves-Brooks would often call upon Percy's services. Percy had a new car every two years and was a great fan of what we then called station wagons – estate cars with genuine wood surrounds on the rear body of the car. The Morris Oxford was Percy's favourite, and he seldom pushed his motors to more than forty miles an hour. But as I got to know Ronnie Brooks better, there was no need to have worried about his views on Percy's 'damned Daz,' for he was used to a bit of fruity language and had a wicked sense of humour.

A Varsity blue at football in his younger days – he played on the wing – the rector often travelled to Kenilworth Road to watch Luton Town's matches. On such occasions, he never wore his clerical collar. After a few visits he got to

160

*A Bow Brickhill Youth Club social gathering held at the village school in the late 1940s.*

know the regular supporters around him and asked one of them what he did for a living. 'Bloody farmer, mate', he was told and his companion then went into a very Anglo-Saxon description of life on his farm. 'What about you?' Ronnie was then asked. 'Rector, Bow Brickhill' came the reply. 'Well bugger me!' gasped his new friend, almost, but not quite, lost for words!

I remember the rector once tried to persuade my father-in-law, George, to pretend to be the Bishop of Mombassa. Ronnie wanted Pop, as I called George, to dress in flowing robes and with his tanned complexion and a false beard, pass himself off at a church fete as a visiting foreign cleric. But Pop would have none of it, though the rector did prove to me that there was a decided village grapevine.

Chatting one day over his favourite tipple, a small sherry, Ronnie said that gossip could spread like wildfire through the village. I thought he was pulling my leg when he said that to prove it, next time I delivered my fruit and veg to a certain house at the top of the hill, I should mention that it was a shame we were to lose the rector, now that he had been made Canon of Chichester. He guaranteed, he said, that by the time I reached customers at the bottom end of the village, about an hour or so later, they would by asking me if I'd heard the news. Well, I didn't believe him, but went along with it, and he was absolutely right!

The Wheatsheaf was one of two pubs in the village then, and though that still remains, the other hostelry, The Plough, run as I have mentioned earlier by Jack and Nellie Foulkes and standing next door to the Church Hall, closed down in the early 1960s. It became a private house and its new owners were Charlie and Selina Trotman and their family, who moved from Burrows Close in Woburn Sands. Charlie was a strong union man with the Post Office and a regular visitor to his new home was Robert Maxwell. Maxwell went on to be Labour MP for Buckingham before becoming exposed as a ruthless newspaper tycoon who plundered his employees' pension fund and losing his life at sea in somewhat strange circumstances.

The Wheatsheaf was home to Eustace and Mary Stone and, as well as running the pub, Eustace and his brother Syd, who also lived in the village,

*Acting as navigator to my new father-in-law, George Whittaker, as we set off on a North Bucks motor club rally in 1957.*

operated a small timber business from an adjoining barn-cum-workshop. Syd also had a smallholding which occupied two parcels of land throughout the 1950s and 1960s. One was a small field next to the railway line and fronting the road by the station, the other larger paddock was at the top of the village next to where Edwin Close now stands.

For many years Bow Brickhill appeared content to be regarded as a somewhat isolated village, midway between Fenny Stratford and Woburn Sands, and though it had a train service, there were no buses. Walking to surrounding villages was still quite the accepted thing, though most people had bikes, and gradually more and more villagers moved to owning cars. Certainly the community of perhaps 500 or so in the 1950s was very close knit, with many families, such as the Wests, Bardens, Morris, Odells and Gilks to name but some, able to trace their ancestry back in the village for many, many years. My wife's paternal grandmother was a Gilks, and her brother, Alf, Donald's father, worked for a long time at Miss Garratt's farm just over the railway crossing. The farm boasted a beautiful thatched farmhouse, demolished to make way for the present development on the site. The Dickens brothers also farmed in this area, which is the hamlet of Caldecote.

Sharp-eyed readers will note that my spelling of that hamlet's name is with only one 't' whereas since the advent of Milton Keynes in 1967, the Development Corporation decided to spell it as Caldecotte. It would seem that over the years different periods of time have used either spelling, the one 't' being prevalent from the war years. Not that a different spelling would cut much ice with many of the offspring of the family's mentioned above, who no doubt still pronounce it the North Bucks dialect-cum-Brickhill way, where it is shortened and is said as Caw-cut.

It was one of the first idiosyncracies of Bow Brickhill speech that I was to come across, for I found words like 'claypered' (to be covered in dirt or mud); 'clared' – pronounced cla-a-hed (to be rushing about); and, most baffling of all, 'hotchle' (to move an object from one place to another and pronounced by dropping the aitch) in general, everyday use. I knew, naturally, of North Bucks dialect with its dipthonged vowels particularly, but it was the first time I had

*Miss Garratt's fine old thatched farmhouse at Caldecote. My wife's uncle Alf worked on the farm for many years.*

heard such specific words used within the speech form. I found it fascinating.

Talking about this aspect of village life with my old school chum at Aspley Heath School in the 1940s, Denis Gurner, recently, he remembers some of the words being used by his mother when he was a small boy. He also came up with another, the verb 'to criddle', which is seems, means to hang on to the last drop of tea in your cup. He was often told by his Mum, he says, to 'stop criddling, boy, and give us your cup!' Denis went on to school in Wolverton after the war and, following his National Service, where he qualified as a pilot, he joined the Diplomatic Wireless Service and spent much of his career at Hanslope. We discussed other Bucks-word usage such as 'aggled' (crotchety); 'hommocks' (feet); 'quilter' (big, as in blackberries – They're some quilters!); 'slommuck' (an untidy, dishevelled person); and 'tiggle' (tiggling about meant to tidy up). Denis lived in Downham Road, Woburn Sands, as a boy and remembers it as an unmade road, not metalled over until well into the 1960s.

By 1959 Bow Brickhill was also getting in on the expansion act. In what was the old army camp field on the Woburn Sands road, council houses had been built soon after the war. Now, Downsview appeared, a cul-de-sac development halfway down Station Road, and further council houses had been built opposite Tilbrook Farm. Within a few years Greenways, a selection of self-build plots, would make its appearance, more houses appeared beyond us in the cottage in London Lane, and by 1967, the sharp corner toward Woburn Sands was realigned – the lime trees now on the corner were on the other side of the road, originally – and Edwin Close was built in the former garden and orchard of the Deyns family home, demolished to make way for the realignment.

In 1959, with the rector as President, the village football team was re-formed after an absence of some years and we played matches in one of Don Burgess' fields along the Woburn Sands road. We won the first game 15-3 against a Bletchley Territorial Army side and finished about midway in the table. Ken Burton, who was to manage the side for many years from then on, thought that the team needed strengthening and midway through that first season sought players from outside the village. Ken and I got on very well but I confess this move worried me, and I said so. My view, as chairman, was that

*Bow Brickhill school before extensive alterations were undertaken in the 1960s. To give better access an old chapel, just in picture, right, which was then being used as a factory producing cake wrappings, was demolished.*

*The retirement in 1955 of Miss M.M.Farnsworth, who taught at Bow Brickhill School for many years. Miss Farnsworth lodged with my wife's aunt and uncle, Alf and Lily Gilks, and this photograph shows her with her last class after being presented with a handbag. Also pictured, at the back, to the right, is Mrs J.Illingworth, who was then headmistress.*

*The first season for Bow Brickhill FC after the side was strengthened in 1959 by the inclusion of Woburn Sands boys. Pictured prior to their game at Brickhill against Towcester Reserves are, back row, left-to right: John Sanders, Brian Brewster, Noel Williams, Mick Denton, Alan Fairey, Ted Langridge; front row: Ron Cook, Ted Enever, Stan Robson, Dave Watts, Tony Cook.*

if we had non-village boys playing, could we be sure we would retain their loyalty over a given period? But Ken won the day and that next season, 1960-61, we stormed through our division of the North Bucks league, winning both the knock-out cup and the division title.

The cup-winning side against opponents, Grendon, was certainly a good one but contained only two Bow Brickhill men, John Sanders, who farmed land on the Woburn side of the woods, and Tony Cook, who played outside-left. There was one lad from Little Brickhill, Eric Whiting, at centre-forward, but the remainder were all Woburn Sands based. The match line-up was: John West; Ted Langridge (capt), Alan Fairey; John Sanders, Brian Brewster, John Soave; Maurice Circuitt, Tom Sneddon, Eric Whiting, David Watts, Tony Cook.

The undoubted strength was there in the three key areas. In goal John West was superb, having been on Northampton Town's books and Alan Fairey was an overlapping full-back long before they were fashionable; at centre-half Brian Brewster seemed to have all the time in the world and made it look easy; up front Dave 'Nogger' Watts was dubbed by the local press as the Jimmy Greaves of North Bucks and seemed never to stop scoring goals. Dave's tally that season was 62. I remember around Christmas time telling him I would buy him anything he liked from the spirits shelf at the Bedford Arms if he hit 60. Well, he did it; and he kept me up to buying his drink!

Born in Kings Lynn, Norfolk, in 1942, Dave came with his parents, Wally and Mary, to Woburn Sands in 1946. Mary was a cousin of Mr Markwell, who owned the grocer's shop at the top of Downham Road, and Wally worked there for many years, moving to the Co-op in Newton Road, Bletchey, when Mr Markwell retired. Dave reckons only about half-a-dozen people now refer to him as 'Nogger' – I confess I'm one of them – and he was given the tag when first apprenticed as a cabinet maker at Wolverton Works. On the day he started in 1958, a man with the same surname, and who was nicknamed 'Nogger', retired. The lads on the shop floor duly passed the name on to the new boy with the name of Watts. As Michael Caine is often supposed to remark: 'Not a lot of people know that!'

Dave, Brian and Alan Fairey were duly snapped up by Bletchley United the

*Dave 'Nogger' Watts, dubbed in 1961 by Warren Potter, the sports editor of the Bletchley Gazette, as 'the Jimmy Greaves of North Bucks.' In this picture, taken at New Bradwell that year, Dave is wearing the club's new strip, white with red facings.*

next season, so confirming my fears of losing non-village boys, and when United merged with Bletchley Town, that became their new club. 'Nogger' went on to play for Wolverton Town and Newport Pagnell before hanging up his boots in 1977 and has a soft spot for Bow Brickhill, where, he says, it all began.

Barbara and I were by 1961 young parents with a one year old son, Mark, and finding the cottage a little cramped. My drumming days came to an end when I sold the kit to one of the Lunnon boys at Woburn Sands who was playing in a rock group, for there was now no place to store them, the small bedroom becoming Mark's nursery. Then two cottages opposite The Plough came up for sale and father-in-law, cousin Don, some professional help and myself set to gutting them and converting the two into one.

Dave Watts gave me a hand with the initial labouring and as walls came down we finished up with a pile of rubble in the back garden some fifteen feet high. We managed to get rid of it by offering it free to the local farmers to use as hardcore for their field gateways. We laboured for nearly ten months but in April 1962 our new home was ready, thanks to the unstinting help we had from friends and neighbours. Charlie Trotman did all the electrics, Eddie Chesse made the stairs and hung all the doors, cousin Don did the plumbing, Percy Bonner, a well known Bletchley bricklayer and a mate of father-in-law, did all the bricking and plastering.

For my part I mixed cement, made the tea; painted, made the tea; fetched Percy's bricks, made the tea; unloaded Eddie's wood, made the tea. You can see I played a very important role in the rebuilding process! Finally, it was all done to The Management's satisfaction – I still refer lightheartedly to Barbara by that title even now, and I think she quite likes it. We screwed a nameplate reading 'April Cottage' to the wall of our new home when we moved in. It was a comfortable place and its style actually prompted one village youngster, Terry Hall, to say it looked like a film star's house! But it did have a particular quirk.

We put Mark in the third bedroom at the back of the house but after a few months Barbara asked me if we could move him into the second bedroom at the front. I remember looking at her and saying: 'So you've noticed it as well, then?' It seems that both of us sensed that when we were reading him a

*April Cottage, Bow Brickhill – a photograph taken in March 2002, some 40 years after we made the two cottages into one. The plaque set into the wall just under the roof tells that Bow Brickhill Heath was awarded to the poor of the Parish in 1795 and an Act of Parliament was passed allowing the Trustees to sell it in 1844.*

173

bedtime story, we felt that someone was standing in the doorway watching us. Certainly nothing seemed to interrupt Mark's slumbers but the room always seemed chillier than the rest of the house. And there were instances when we would go out and return to find ornaments teetering on the edges of shelves and cushions from the settee on the floor. Initially we put this down to vibration from traffic going up and down the hill or Riff having games with the cushions. But when it happened during the bad winter of that year, when no traffic could get up the hill, and when Riff wasn't in the house, we realised that we probably had an uninvited guest!

Mark was duly moved to the second bedroom, and I used that back room as an office-cum-study. Riff slept in there at night with no problems at all. The unexplained events with the ornaments and cushions lessened but didn't stop altogether, though by the early Spring of 1963 we were to move again, not because of any of the experiences in April Cottage, but because the Misses Frost wanted to retire and said they would like us to buy their shop, The Pines, just fifty yards down the road. April Cottage sold quickly enough to a couple from Bedford, Jack and Olive Kingston, who had no children. They made further alterations internally and when we told them of our experiences, they looked at us a little in disbelief because, they said, nothing seemed untoward to them. They invited us back one day for a cup of tea, and we went upstairs and stood in the back bedroom. It was no longer chilly and the atmosphere was totally different. Whatever was there, if there was anything, had gone completely.

Over the years Barbara and I have come to the conclusion that in renovating the cottages we disturbed a poltergeist or something – poltergeists are often attracted to little children, it seems – but when we sold the house to a childless couple, it went away.

Before moving on there is one little tale I must tell of that nasty winter of 1962/63. Before the hill became totally impassable, either up or down, one of the village lads was in Woburn with his car. As the afternoon light faded quickly it began to snow heavily, so he made for home. In the gathering gloom he was more intent on following the road than anything else and completely forgot to switch on the car's lights. Followed by a police car all the way from Woburn, through the woods and on to the church, he was then pulled over. Referring to his lack of illumination, the police officer asked him: 'Now, Sir, what should we have on in this weather?' 'Wellingtons!' said the lad, quick as a flash!

We did the deal with Maggie and Thurza and moved into The Pines just a year and a day after we had moved in to April Cottage. Once more we went through the ritual of stripping out, repairing and remaking, painting and decorating. Pop was up on a thick wooden plank painting the stairs one evening when cousin Don arrived to help out. Looking at the plank Donald told him: 'You're alright there, then, chap! That'll never break!' He turned away to get his own paint and brushes and within seconds there was a mighty crack, the plank snapping clean in two and sending poor George sprawling across the stairs with white gloss paint all over his face, in his hair, in his pockets and in his shoes. Luckily he was unhurt and saw the funny side of it, for it took him some time to stop laughing and report back to mother-in-law in his sorry state. Apparently, as he opened the door to confront her, she just asked, in good Bucks style: 'Pray, man, whatever have you been at now; you're claypered in paint!'

A couple of weeks later it was Donald's turn to be the butt of a giggle. In renovating the floor of the shop, Pop and I found one of the joists rotting away. Still, it was a simple repair: cut out the bad timber and replace it with a new piece.

A chunk of four by two was soon nailed on to bridge the gap left by the cutaway timber. Looking at it from above, you couldn't see the two ends of the four by two so a repair wasn't obvious. In wanders Donald, looks into the hole and says very seriously: 'Ah, look at them joists. They don't put 'em in like that nowadays. Last years they will...' Pop and I just looked at each other and said nothing, but we did tell him later!

Though we modernised the shop and the round was still doing well, it soon became clear that we had made a mistake in taking on the extra commitment. We knew we were doing more business than the Misses Frost, but it was still nowhere near what we had hoped.

Within eighteen months we decided to cut our losses completely. We would close down the shop, turn the business accommodation into extra living quarters, and I would give up the round and try and find a job back in

*Miss M.M.Farnsworth, nearest camera, with Thurza Frost, Maggie Frost and on the right, Lily Gilks, at a Bow Brickhill produce show. It was from the Frost sisters that we were to buy The Pines.*

*The Pines, Church Road, Bow Brickhill, as it is today. The car is parked in front of what was on the right of the building; the original shop front was in front of what was our original sitting room.*

journalism. A bigger, brighter, better Bletchley was by now as its peak and two shops in the town, coupled with the growing mobility of people, were having an effect on small traders, such as us, in the villages. The two shops were Elmo and Fine Fare. The first one-stop supermarkets had arrived.

Within the two supermarkets housewives found they could buy all the groceries, fruit, veg and household sundries they needed under one roof, and you could park close by in Bletchley Road and so do all your shopping in one fell swoop. As well as the convenience factor, the purchasing power of these new big stores meant that they could retail their goods for less than small shopkeepers like us could buy wholesale. It was a phenomenal social change that was to gather momentum over the years and sound the death knell for most village traders.

By the late autumn of 1964 we had closed down the shop and I telephoned Carl Moser on the Bletchley Gazette to see if he had any editorial vacancies. He hadn't, he said, but he knew someone who did have, and he would make a telephone call on my behalf. Within two days I had heard from the proprietor of the Bucks Standard at Newport Pagnell, a Mr Crawford Macgregor Hercus, who lived then on Aspley Heath. We met on a Thursday evening in The Swan Hotel at Woburn Sands, and I started work for him as a reporter ten days later. I was back in full-time journalism and determined now, at the age of thirty, to make a career of it.

On the home front we stripped out all the shop fittings and sold them off – my former cycle speedway club president Don Sewell had one of the big chest freezers, I recall – and made the shop area into a proper hallway, second sitting room and a separate dining room. I determined to find time to really get the very large garden to rights, so after I had started work at the Bucks Standard I planted new fruit trees, cut out flower beds and added to the stock of chickens and ducks kept in The Pines' sizeable orchard.

Most of this was done at weekends as, no longer self- employed, I couldn't snatch the odd hour off to garden as I used to. But it seemed to work out alright and I found I still had time to play football for Brickhill, enjoy my rough shooting over Don Burgess' fields with both gun or hunting bow and arrows

*Bletchley Road, Bletchley, in 1963. The Fine Fare supermarket is shown, left; the Elmo supermarket was on the other side of the road, towards the station, on the site now occupied by the Somerfield's store.*

and go early morning fishing on some Sundays with Dick Robinson, a very keen angler who lived just a few doors away. If ever you want to feel at peace with the world, then I can thoroughly recommend a spot of fishing on a warm, summer Sunday morning on a quiet stretch of water. Church bells in the distance, a hot flask of coffee, and maybe a pipe of tobacco – bliss, sheer bliss.

# CHAPTER 8

# THE GENESIS OF MILTON KEYNES

With my mobile shop now replaced by a black, secondhand Triumph Herald car, I drove to Newport Pagnell each day to work in the tiny offices of the Bucks Standard in Silver Street. The quickest way from Bow Brickhill then was via Walton, Milton Keynes village, Broughton and into Newport via Tickford Street, and a pleasant ride through the country it was, too. At the office I found only one other editorial member of staff, a friendly lady named Pat Lett whose husband, Ken, had his own building firm based in Emberton, I believe. Pat was well known in Newport and as Pat Loxley, before she married, was an excellent hockey player, playing alongside Guin Parker, from Woburn Sands, in the Bletchley ladies hockey team. Pat was a Jill-of-all-trades as far as the Bucks Standard went. She was a trained monotype operator, so she set much of the type, she sub-edited my copy and designed the pages, and at times she even sold advertising! She was, in everything but title, the editor.

I soon settled back into the weekly newspaper routine. Monday was catching up on the weekend's events, not least on the sporting scene, and getting them written up. With no staff photographer the Bucks Standard relied on a supply of pictures from established photographic studios, such as Derek Snow, of Newport Pagnell, and news freelance photographers in the mould of Ivor Leonard, from Bletchley, a former Gazette photographer who, with his partner John Flewin, was then running the highly successful Three Counties news agency, based in John's home on the outskirts of Newton Longville. By the middle of the week the Bucks Standard office would be supplied with any relevant papers pertinent to council committee and full council meetings of the three local authorities in whom the Standard had an interest – Newport Pagnell Urban District Council, with offices just around the corner in the High Street, Newport Pagnell Rural, whose area went right out to Olney in one direction and Woburn Sands and my own Bow Brickhill in the other, and

Wolverton Urban District Council which covered Stony Stratford and as well, of course, Wolverton itself. So on the local government scene I was kept pretty busy almost from day one with both daytime and evening meetings.

Thursday was court day at Newport while Friday was court day at Stony Stratford. The Bucks Standard was printed late on a Friday morning and if there was a court case of any note at Stony Stratford, we would try and hold up the printing until early afternoon so that we could carry the story. In this way we gave our readers up to the minute news and at the same time beat our rivals, The Wolverton Express, to the punch, for the Express printed on Thursday afternoons.

I remember that it was at Newport court in, I think, my very first week of work that I came across a man called Bernard Ringham. Bernard was a good reporter who covered the district for the Northampton evening paper, the Chronicle and Echo, but I don't think he was the nicest bloke I've ever met. He struck me as being somewhat self-important and whenever there was an audience, took great delight in talking down to people of some standing, such as the magistrates at court, higher ranking officers in the police, council officials and especially members or prospective members of parliament. In fact, he didn't talk down to them; he was just downright rude.

He had a go at me at our first meeting at court for the way I was dressed. Now for nine years I had been used to wearing for my work what we would now call casual wear, and that always meant an open-necked shirt, summer and winter. I was never a great lover of ties, which I found restricting – and I still don't like them now – so when I began at the Bucks Standard I wore sports coat and flannels, shirt and a cravat, instead of a tie, just to neaten the neckline. Well, as far as Mr Ringham was concerned, you would have thought I had turned up in beggar's rags. He tried to give me a stern lecture on the way to dress for court, and it became clear that he knew about my background. 'You're not on your barrow boy's cart, now!' he told me. That was enough. He was a somewhat overweight little fellow and I told him in no uncertain terms to mind his own business or he might sport a bruise or two. He seemed to give me a wide berth after that and, though I did wear ties on occasions, if I knew he was going to be around, then I purposely wore a cravat!

One of the big local government issues of the time was the continued expansion of Bletchley and the possibility of some even larger, planned development for the area. Bletchley made no secret of the fact that it wanted its bigger, brighter, better slogan carried through to encompass anything beyond its own boundaries in which it might be involved, and saw itself as the automatic centre of affairs should this sort of expansion occur.

From earlier in the 1960s, and looking at the county plan, Bucks County Council produced a series of policy reports which culminated in a 'Strategic Planning Policy, 1964-81.' From this, in September 1962, a 'New city report, number 2' was produced and an expansion strategy explored in the light of the London overspill population problem. Feasibility studies showed that a population of 250,000 was a possibility should a new city be built in the north of the county and that the running costs of its proposed public transport system – a monorail – should be borne out of the rates, or what we would now call council tax. The monorail idea was the brainchild of the County Council's highly talented chief architect Fred Pooley, and the concept of a new city in the Bletchley – Wolverton area quickly became known as 'Pooleyville.'

Two months later, report three suggested that if such development took place, the walking distance from a monorail station should be no more than seven minutes and small townships within the city could be of 5,000-7,000 people.

In January, 1964, another report – called this time 'County of Buckingham Development Plan Review'- was submitted to the county planning committee and adopted by the full council in the following May. Among its positive aims were the construction of a new city for 250,000 in the north of the county, together with major expansions for existing towns. An appendix to the report showed how the new city could be built to cope with the car. It was provisionally planned as an oval-shaped conurbation, with its two ends or points at Bletchley in the south and Wolverton in the north. However, these initial planning thoughts did see problems with the water supply and sewage disposal, just as had the Abercrombie report nearly twenty years earlier.

Within a couple of weeks of my joining the Bucks Standard in early

November 1964, the County Council had firmed up its ideas and its planning committee came up with its own definitive proposals. To everyone's surprise, though, Bletchley was shown as being outside the proposed development boundary.

The new city, as it was now most positively referred to by the planning committee in its report to the County Council, would be built on virgin soil between Bletchley in the south and Wolverton in the north, extending east to west from the M1 motorway to Beachampton and Nash. Pinched in at the waist, its centre would be based on Loughton, and it was soon dubbed Loughton city. In a lengthy preamble to its report, the Council's planning committee stressed these were only proposals within a framework of ongoing consultations between itself and central government with regard to a study of the south-east of England, and a report commissioned by Government on the relationship of such proposals to proposed development at Bedford and Northampton.

The preamble went on: 'Although, therefore, your committee are not yet able to make any recommendation leading to a final decision by the Council to proceed with the proposal, they nevertheless feel strongly that it is desirable to maintain the impetus beyond this all-important proposal and to advance matters to the stage where the Council will be in a position to go ahead at short notice with the reservation and acquisition of the necessary land, once the financial and practicable feasibility of the scheme has been established in the light of the discussions and investigations which are ongoing and the decision to be reached by Government.'

In short, then, although the County Council was covering its own back and ready for disappointment, it was clear that people in very high places were casting serious developmental eyes over our North Bucks countryside. The day when our farming communities and rural environment were to be under threat could not be very far away.

In October 1966, the same year that HM Queen Elizabeth visited Bletchley and Bletchley Road became Queensway to mark the occasion, the Ministry of Housing and Local Government published its own report on the proposed developments.

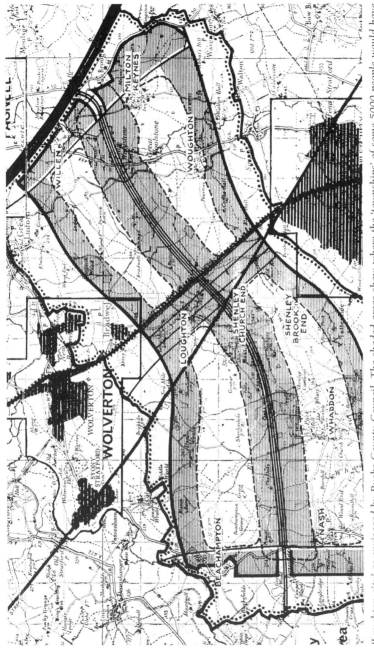

'Loughton city' as envisaged by Bucks County Council. The shaded areas show where the 'townships' of some 5000 people would have been located, the white areas were to be used as open spaces to provide areas for parks, playing fields and some farming. The city centre, taking in Loughton, is seen mainly between the A5 Watling Street and the railway line. The M1 is the thick black line, top right.

This looked at the inter-relationship of Bedford and Northampton's expansion to any proposed development in North Bucks -just as the County Council envisaged – and the recommended area in North Bucks for large scale development, shown in a map published in December, put Bletchley back in the frame as an integral part of any new city. Bletchley councillors were delighted, even though the new city proposals would cause obvious problems for the town's own planning aspirations. The National Farmers Union, however, was less than pleased.

Firmly opposed to the loss of vast tracts of excellent farmland to the steel tracks of the bulldozer and consequent layers of concrete, the NFU mounted a vigorous protest against the now almost certain development when around 150 farmers met at Water Eaton in January 1966. I covered the meeting for the Bucks Standard with colleagues from the other local newspapers. We learned that not least among the NFU concerns were the pitiful rates of compensation then payable to tenant farmers who lost their livelihood because of enforced development. Under the chairmanship of Bill Snook, who farmed at Water Eaton, a steering committee was formed with the particular aim, among others, of getting revised and better terms on the statute book. It was to take some time for that particular aspect to be resolved. At the end of the day, Bill Snook and his committee won through but not before I had nailed the Bucks Standard's colours firmly to the NFU mast and, in more than one story, predicted a land grab should plans become official.

Two months before the farmers held their meeting at Water Eaton, Councillor Jim Cassidy, of Bletchley UDC, told Fenny Stratford parishioners that although Bletchley had expanded rapidly since the war, no-one could be proud of what had been achieved. His view, he said, was that the planned expansion to date had created a one-class town and that there was now an urgent need for more than just factory jobs. He said that Bletchley should encourage electronic, computer, technical and service industries to the town, and if this sort of expansion did not come, then all Bletchley offered was a place to live with your children. His vision of the future was practically a blue-print of what was to come in the shape of Milton Keynes.

In June of 1966 I moved on from the Bucks Standard to join my former chief reporter on the North Bucks Times, Tom Milligan, on the sub-editor's table at the Bedfordshire Times. I thought I was ready to progress after some eighteen months back at the chalk face and the vacancy at the table, which gave me direct responsibilities in relation to the Woburn Reporter, which circulated in Aspley Guise and Woburn Sands, was too good an opportunity to miss.

As well as the professional realities, the job also paid more than I was getting at Newport Pagnell, and Barbara was expecting our second child within weeks. Against this flurry of personal activity, of course, the question of a new town in the area was almost the sole topic of conversation.

On 18 July 1966, our daughter, Rachel, was born at The Pines. I remember some pleasant late summer and early autumn days that year and Rachel would snooze quietly in her pram in the garden, watched over by Riff who, being the pretty hefty fellow that he was, would stick his head over the rim of the pram and tell us all was well by a wag of his tail. Then, just before Christmas that year, I had another offer I couldn't refuse. Mr Hercus telephoned me to ask if I was interested in going back to the Bucks Standard as editor in my own right, with a completely free hand and with powers of hire and fire. I didn't hesitate, and began in the New Year.

Within almost a few days of returning to Silver Street, all the doubts and innuendo about a new city were finally laid to rest. A draft designation order was published by the Ministry of Housing and Local Government and the new development was to take its name from one of the smallest villages within the designated area. Milton Keynes was now a reality. In excess of 25,000 acres of land was to be used to build the new city – bigger than Fred Pooley's monorail concept by some 2000 acres – and the overall development would be under the control of a quasi-autonomous national government organisation (quango) to be titled the Milton Keynes Development Corporation.

By April of 1967 the Board to which the officers of the Corporation would report was set up and included local representatives such as Jim Cassidy from Bletchley UDC, Ray Bellchambers from Newport Pagnell RDC, and Margaret Durbridge, a Newport Pagnell magistrate and the town's County Council representative. The Labour peer, Lord Campbell of Eskan, became chairman of the Board and it met for the first time on 15 June 1967 at Milton Keynes village hall. Four days earlier, on the Monday of that week, Lord Campbell had carried out at Water Eaton the ceremony of cutting the first turf in the development of Milton Keynes. Ironically, it was right outside Bill Snook's farm, though as events were to unfold, the building bulk of the city was to have little physical effect on Water Eaton itself. Headquarters were set up at Wavendon Tower – a stone's throw outside the city's designated area – and Walter Ismay, an able and very likable man, came out of Yorkshire Imperial Metals, where he was director and chief engineer, to become deputy chairman of the Board and full time chief executive of the Corporation.

I found it a rewarding time with a lot of job satisfaction, for on the Milton Keynes front Walter Ismay was proving a good friend to the local press. Along with John Baker, from the Bletchley Gazette, I would often meet up at Wavendon Tower for a briefing update from Walter.

It was at such a briefing that we were to meet the first of the senior officers of the Corporation as they came on board – Ernest Pye, the engineer; George Whitaker, the admin. officer; and a man who was much admired by us all but sadly died while still comparatively young, Alan Ashton, the estates officer. Plans for the overall development of the city were prepared by several agencies but the firm of Llwellyn-Davies, Weekes, Forestier-Walker and Bor eventually won the day and Fred Pooley, from Bucks County Council, became Lord Campbell's consultant.

While all this was taking place, keeping me busy and continually in the headlines of all the local papers, there were other things I wanted to do with the Bucks Standard. First was to rejig the content of the newspaper to give it a more modern image, so the sports pages went from page two to the back and inside back, the centre pages became special feature pages for items of local interest, typefaces were changed to give a more modern look and most importantly, I believe, I introduced 'Viewpoint' – an editorial column in which I tried to give an in depth, and where possible unbiased, appraisal of local topics.

It seemed to work and sales began to increase little by little. I was joined

*Our last home in Bow Brickhill, 4 Edwin Close, which we moved to in 1967. We were to stay there until October 1985, when we moved to our present home in Bletchley.*

by two juniors, Jane Hunt, the daughter of the manager of Newport Pagnell's Co-op, and Jon Hill, who came from Buckingham, and in late 1967, with the job going very well, Barbara and I sold The Pines to move into the new development created by the realignment of the road as it left Bow Brickhill for Woburn Sands. Five houses were put up by Edwin Clark, a Harpenden builder, four in a line, the fifth coming later when Mr Clark found there was room for one more. Go into Edwin Close, as it was so-named after himself by Mr Clark, for it is a private road still, and you will find the house numbers run five, then one, two, three, four. We moved in to number four and were to stay there until we moved to our present home in Bletchley in 1985.

By 1968 the Bucks Standard was going great guns and it was then that Mr Hercus came to me and asked how much did I know about the printing process called web-offset. The answer to that was very little, but the composing room staff, headed by a man named John James, who lived in Stony Stratford, were already beginning to use newer, lithographic techniques to produce some of the paper's advertising copy and a small amount of my editorial material. So John and I got together – John did most of the talking because he was a production man – and eventually we were able to go to Mr Hercus with a programme of reorganisation if he wanted to install a web-offset printing press in place of the old, flat sheet press we were then using.

I will not go into the intricacies of offset-litho production and web-offset techniques here, save to say that we went ahead with the system in Newport Pagnell to become the first local newspaper in the area to use the technique. It gave us a clarity of print and photographs that no-one else could match, and I began to use a higher proportion of photographs than I had before as we boosted the newspaper's pagination.

I recall Alan Ashton telephoning me about this time and inviting me to lunch at The Swan, at Milton Keynes, for a chat about the role of the rivers and the canal that were an integral part of the designated area. In my editorials I had been more than a little scathing about the overall development costing North Bucks its farming industry and its rural environment, and Alan said he thought a working lunch might give me a useful story.

Alan briefed me on the overall objective for Milton Keynes to be open-plan with lots of greenery, and the rivers and the canal becoming the mainstays of a series of linear parks that would criss-cross the city. As the development went on, he said, the Corporation would plant literally millions of trees and shrubs to enhance the environment, and wherever possible, existing trees and hedgerows would be kept. At the end of the meal I had my story, but I confess I was a little sceptical, telling Alan: 'I've yet to meet a builder who's a gardener or who gives a fig for the environment. Pull the other leg, Alan, it's got bells on!'

I went back to the Bucks Standard office and wrote the story up as a centre-spread feature, that is to say it occupied the two middle pages completely. The headline I put across the top read: 'City of trees...' and it is a phrase still used today to describe Milton Keynes. Alan was right, and I was wrong to doubt him, for although we have lost our farming industry, I believe that if anything, the Development Corporation enhanced the overall environment of the area. All of the canal, some of which was inaccessible to the public because it bordered private land, has become open to us, and the linear parks themselves are a joy to look at and experience at any time of the year. The ancient woodlands are now properly managed, and there is no finer sight than Howe Park wood in March, April and May when first the primroses, then the bluebells, are in full bloom. Alan's department has planted the millions of trees and shrubs that he promised and I am sad only about one thing. I never had the chance to shake Alan's hand before he died and admit I was wrong.

The main reason for that was that by 1969, and still fired with my enthusiasm for the wonders of web-offset printing, I left the Bucks Standard to work in London. I was to stay there for nearly twenty years, my time culminating with a two year spell as director of public affairs for a professional association.

It was only then, in 1989, that I turned my back on commuting to the capital and became media relations manager for, who else but, the Milton Keynes Development Corporation. By then, of course, Milton Keynes was already the successful city we have today. When the Corporation was wound-up, many say prematurely, by the Secretary of State for the Environment Michael Heseltine, in March 1992, I retired from full time work.

The three-and-a-bit years I had with the Corporation were most enjoyable and culminated in working closely with Royal household and Government staff when the Queen visited Milton Keynes only a week or so before the Corporation closed its doors. Her Majesty signed a portrait for the city that day, which hangs now in the Council Offices. Just before the signing was due to take place, though, it was realised that the Queen only ever uses a traditional fountain pen, and there didn't seem to be one around. By sheer chance I had a fountain pen in my briefcase. My lasting memory of Her Majesty's visit, then, is not just that I was presented, along with the Government press corps when the tour finished at the De Montfort university, but that my pen was used for the portrait signing. And no, it hasn't been used since!

Since the Corporation departed, Milton Keynes has become a unitary authority and as such has taken on many of Bucks County Council's former responsibilities. Many of the people who have assisted in the compilation of this book agree with me that the place deserves its unitary status, but they query whether our Council has the intellectual power and commercial know-how to run it. At very least, the change from borough council to unitary authority is a bit of a quantum leap. However, I must leave my readers to their own conclusions, though perhaps it is not too much to hope that in future, councillors of all parties might be elected for their additional business acumen, not just their political fervour.

The period I have covered within these pages spans almost a quarter of a century. In those years the Bletchley district has undergone such fundamental social and physical change that it makes the advent of the railway in 1838 look small beer. Initially, as I have tried to show, the change was to benefit Bletchley enormously and to expand the range of job opportunities for local people. As the population grew, changing faces went hand in glove with changing places. But now, in the early years of a new century, Bletchley's Queensway is a shadow of its former self, in spite of repeated efforts towards regeneration, and the town has long since relinquished its claim to be the civic and commercial centre of the area. Aspley Guise and Bow Brickhill are like so

*Geoff Tremayne, a very popular headmaster at Bow Brickhill School, pictured with his class in 1968. My son Mark is fourth from left, behind the seated girls.*

many villages now, merely dormitories, with the latter having lost even its Post Office. Woburn Sands seems to have fared better and now enjoys town status but, clearly, Central Milton Keynes rules supreme.

To end, there is one last anecdote I must tell about Milton Keynes, and it concerns its name. For many years throughout the 1970s and 1980s, many people believed that it took its title from the poet Milton or from references to a certain financial guru. I think that myth has been pretty much laid to rest over the years and that everyone now knows that a tiny village, which had less than 200 inhabitants in the 1960s, gave its name to the new development. Some books will tell you that the village name was chosen by Anthony Greenwood, who succeeded Richard Crossman as Minister of Housing and Local Government. Not true; and I will explain why.

When Richard Crossman invited the local press to meet him in Whitehall early in 1967 for the announcement of the new town, four of us made the journey – Bert Foxford, the much respected editor of the Wolverton Express; Harold 'Heppy' Hepworth from Carl Moser's Bletchley Gazette; Bernard Ringham from the Northampton Chronicle and Echo; and myself from the Bucks Standard. In my thirties, I was the baby of the party, and the four of us could claim to be the first of the local public who knew where the development was to go, how big it was going to be, and, more importantly, what it was going to be called. Of the four, I am the only one now left alive.

We all fired our questions at Mr Crossman but no-one asked him his reason for choosing the name Milton Keynes. He told us, of course, that it was to be named after one of the smallest villages in the designated area but, other than that, gave out no information as to what had prompted that choice. So I asked him.

He looked back at me across his desk, adjusted his heavy tortoiseshell-framed spectacles on his nose, and I waited, pencil poised, for some academic or historically based answer. He repeated my question: 'Why Milton Keynes, Mr Enever?' I nodded, almost imperceptibly.

'Because I like the sound of it,' he said. 'I like the sound of it!'

194

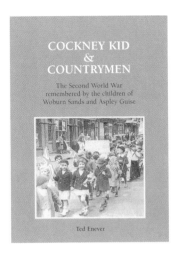

# COCKNEY KID AND COUNTRYMEN
The Second World War remembered by the children
of Woburn Sands and Aspley Guise

### by Ted Enever

On the evening of Saturday 7th September 1940, London's East End lay under a pall of smoke from heavy bombing by the German Luftwaffe. It was the beginning of what history was to record as the Blitz.

Six year old Ted and his parents were victims of that first attack. With home and possessions lost, they left London to find safety, shelter and a new way of life in the villages of Woburn Sands and Aspley Guise.

"Cockney Kid and Countrymen" is Ted Enever's story of that new way of life and a snapshot of the wartime years vividly remembered by the village children of the time.

Ted was educated at Bedford Modern School and entered journalism in 1951 with the Bletchley District Gazette. After two years national service he continued his career as a freelance journalist, with various large organisations. On retirement he was working for Milton Keynes Development Corporation. A founder member of the Bletchley Park Trust and now a Patron, Ted is author of "Britains Best Kept Secret-Ultra's base at Bletchley Park."

A Book Castle Publication

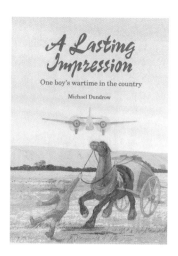

# A LASTING IMPRESSION

## by Michael Dundrow

Michael Dundrow experienced an event in his formative years which strongly coloured or even completely changed the rest of his life.

This book describes one boy's overwhelming experience – wartime evacuation – which has left a truly lasting impression on his adult life. For this twelve year old from London's East End, to be dumped among a family of strangers on a large and busy farm below the Chilterns in Bedfordshire was a make or break experience of the first order.

Enriched by his years on the farm and in the village of Totternhoe, the adventures with new found friends, the sheer interest, fun and hard work of farm life and also the sowing of the seeds of appreciation of that lovely corner of South Bedfordshire, the details are all here, written with great affection. Although written fifty years after these unforgettable things happened, the story is undimmed by the passage of time.

In this evocative picture of wartime England are many glimpses of a way of village and farm life that has altered so dramatically in recent years as to be almost unrecognisable today.

A Book Castle Publication

196

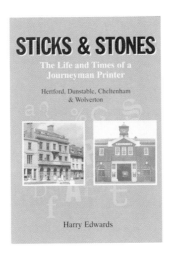

## STICKS & STONES

The Life and Times of a Journeyman Printer
Hertford, Dunstable, Cheltenham & Wolverton

### by Harry Edwards

Sticks and Stones recounts the story of the author's journey through his life in the printing industry, from printer's devil until retirement. Leaving school at the age of fourteen, Harry's transition from schoolboy to apprentice was abrupt. The printing world, with its own language, customs and tradition, was strange at first but most of the journeymen were kind and helpful to a young lad, covering up for many a mistake in the first formative years. The journey begins in Hertfordshire, then takes him on to Bedfordshire, Gloucestershire, London and finally to Buckinghamshire.

A Book Castle Publication

# THREADS OF TIME

## by Sheila Porter

A pale-faced city child is evacuated from London during the Zeppelin raids of 1917. In Hitchin she takes a dressmaking apprenticeship and opens her own workshop with customers including the local gentry and the young Flora Robson.

Moving to Bedford on her marriage, her sewing skills help her rapidly growing family to survive the Depression; working long hours during the exigencies of war-time Britain, it is her re-designed battle-jacket that Glenn Miller is wearing when he disappears over the Channel in 1944, and entertainers Bing Crosby and Bob Hope leave comics and candy for her 'cute kids'. For five years after the war the family run a small café in the town but sewing then sees her through again as the business is sold, she is widowed with a nine-year old son to raise, all her children gradually leave and she moves away to be wardrobe mistress to a big operatic society in High Wycombe. Finally she settles in a small cottage opposite the great airship sheds at Cardington from where she once watched the ill-fated R101 take off on its last journey in 1930. A mirror of her times, this gripping biography tells the story of a remarkable lady, a talented dressmaker, mostly in Hitchin and Bedford – played out against the unfolding drama of the entire twentieth century.

A Book Castle Publication

# GLEANINGS REVISITED

Nostalgic Thoughts of a Bedfordshire Farmer's Boy

## by E.W.O'Dell

The original small town of Barton has gradually spread and grown over the years. Very few of the current residents can still recall the way of life there in days gone by. However, here one of the few collected his thoughts and embellished them with his own sketches, plus early photographs. These are not always idyllic memories, but they are real, they are lively and they give an insight into rural Bedfordshire as many once experienced it – at work, rest and play.

A Book Castle Publication

# HISTORIC FIGURES
# IN THE BUCKINGHAMSHIRE LANDSCAPE
## by John Houghton

For centuries the County of Buckinghamshire has evolved, remaining always pastoral and agricultural. Yet, in terms of national history, Bucks has been no backwater. It has played its part in times of national crisis and upheaval. It has furnished great leaders, whether in politics or in art. It is rich in 'cards and characters' whose eccentricity excites interest. Like any other county, it has its heroes and villains.

The book tells of 100 "figures in a Buckinghamshire landscape". They include: warriors and men-at-arms, statesmen and politicians, literary geniuses, polemicists and agitators, plutocrats and tycoons, plotters and regicides and some ordinary folk who did ordinary things! These 100 individuals were as diverse as could be. What links them all is that Bucks was their county, either by birth or by adoption.

In the final chapter there are a further 7,000 "figures in a Buckinghamshire landscape" – they are the Code Breakers of Bletchley Park.

A Book Castle Publication

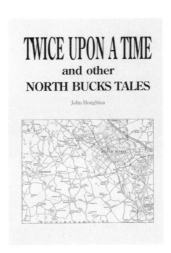

## TWICE UPON A TIME
### and other
## NORTH BUCKS TALES

### by John Houghton

Fifteen stories that are tales of fiction with a touch of fact. But the places are all real and are all to be found in North Bucks.

Some of the people who appear in the book were real historical characters... Sir Edmund Verney for example, who lost his life at the battle of Edgehill in 1642. And John Bunyan, the travelling tinker, who wrote 'Pilgrim's Progress'. And Thomas Adams of Swanborne, who was murdered 'on Liscombe ground' near Soulbury in 1626.

But all the other characters that appear in these pages are imaginary. And any likeness to actual persons is coincidental.

A Book Castle Publication

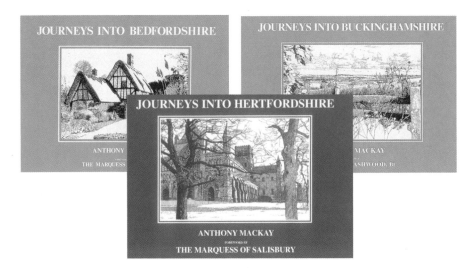

# JOURNEYS INTO BEDFORDSHIRE
# JOURNEYS INTO BUCKINGHAMSHIRE
# JOURNEYS INTO HERTFORDSHIRE

### by Anthony Mackay

These three books of ink drawings reveal an intriguing historic heritage and capture the spirit of England's rural heartland, ranging widely over cottages and stately homes, over bridges, churches and mills, over sandy woods, chalk downs and watery river valleys.

Every corner of Bedfordshire, Buckinghamshire and Hertfordshire has been explored in the search for material, and, although the choice of subjects is essentially a personal one, the resulting collection represents a unique record of the environment today.

The notes and maps, which accompany the drawings, lend depth to the books, and will assist others on their own journeys around the counties.

Anthony Mackay's pen-and-ink drawings are of outstanding quality. An architectural graduate, he is equally at home depicting landscapes and buildings. The medium he uses is better able to show both depth and detail than any photograph.

A Book Castle Publication